P9-DMB-428

EVA

EVA

THE REAL KEY TO CREATING WEALTH

AL EHRBAR

John Wiley & Sons, Inc.
New York • Chichester • Weinheim • Brisbane • Singapore • Toronto

This book is printed on acid-free paper. ♾

Published by John Wiley & Sons, Inc.
Published simultaneously in Canada.

Library of Congress Cataloging-in-Publication Data:

Ehrbar, Al.
EVA : the real key to creating wealth / Al Ehrbar.
p. cm.
Includes index.
ISBN 0-471-29860-3 (cloth : alk. paper)
1. Economic value added. I. Title.
HG4028.V3E367 1998
658.15—dc21 98-11704

Printed in the United States of America.

10 9 8 7 6 5 4 3 2 1

Contents

Acknowledgments

I would like to say that the ideas presented in this book are my own. Most anyone would. In fact, my role has mostly been that of translator and explicator. The EVA concept, and the financial management and incentive compensation systems built around it, reflect the contributions of many brilliant individuals. The best I can claim is the acquaintanceship of all of them and the friendship of many. I am greatly indebted to them for what they have taught me—and what I hope I have communicated adequately in these pages—about the essential matter of wealth creation.

As Joel M. Stern explains in the Foreword that follows, the theoretical genesis of EVA is found in the economic model of the value of the firm developed by Nobel laureates Merton H. Miller and Franco Modigliani. EVA also owes much to the pathbreaking work on organizational behavior and agency costs by Michael C. Jensen and the late William H. Meckling, two professors I had the good fortune to study under at the University of Rochester. Bill, in particular, was one of the greatest teachers I have known. His lectures on the theory of the firm provided much more than a solid grounding in microeconomics; they laid out an invaluable framework for analyzing self-interest and motivation in all aspects of life.

The translation of those theoretical breakthroughs into an easily understood system that enables managers to optimally direct the resources of any corporation is principally the work of Joel Stern and G. Bennett Stewart III, the eponymous founders of Stern Stewart & Co. This was no mean feat. Financial economists have long known that costs, properly measured, include a so-called normal return on investment, and that "profits" don't begin until corporations have covered that normal return. This was part of the basic course material in price theory at leading business schools as far back as the late sixties. And we have known for just as long that conventional accounting seriously distorts the true economics of the firm. Grasping those ideas is one thing. Casting them in a way that anyone can understand them and use them in their daily decisions is something else. That Joel and Bennett accomplished it owes to the fact that they have spent their careers—more than half a century between them—making the insights of modern financial theory accessible and useful to operating managers.

The evolution of the EVA system into its present form involved contributions from many other individuals as well. They include, but are not limited to, David M. Glassman, a founding partner of Stern Stewart who has guided the implementation of EVA at scores of companies, Eli Lilly, Boise Cascade, and J.C. Penney among them, and Dennis Soter, the Stern Stewart partner most responsible for the application of EVA principles to financial strategy and balance-sheet structure. Others who deserve special mention are Gregory V. Milano, manager of many EVA projects, including the ones at Telecom New Zealand, Siemens, and Tatetlyle, and now the partner in charge of Stern Stewart's European practice; Justin Pettit, who worked with SPX Corporation and Herman Miller, among others, and John M. Ferguson, director of the Latin American EVA practice. The greatest contributors to the success of EVA, however, are the CEOs and CFOs who have adopted the system, especially the pioneers who had the wisdom to recognize the rightness of it and the courage to embrace it even before my former colleagues at *FORTUNE* gave it their invaluable imprimatur in a cover story by

Shawn Tully (from which I poached the subtitle for this book) five years ago.

I also want to acknowledge several others who helped in the preparation of this book. Irwin Ross and John Goff, friends and colleagues for many years, provided important assistance in the reporting. Tom Leander and Cécile Lefort carried a lot of extra water to free me from many of my regular duties at Stern Stewart and give me the time to write, and my editor at John Wiley & Sons, Mina Samuels, provided guidance that improved both the rhetoric and the organization of this work. Most of all, I thank my wife, Marina, for her patience and encouragement.

Al Ehrbar

New York
July 1998

Foreword

Joel M. Stern

EVA, as a measure of performance, has been a part of the economist's tool kit for more than 200 years. In its most fundamental form, EVA (economic value added) is the simple notion of residual income. That is, for investors to earn an adequate rate of return, the return must be large enough to compensate for risk. Thus, residual income is zero if a firm's operating return is just equal to the required return for risk. Of course, the required return is a capital charge for both debt and equity.

In contrast, the accountant's measure of profit, while also recognizing the need to use residual income, subtracts a required return only for senior securities, the interest cost of debt, and dividends paid on preferred stock. The accountant's residual income, known as net profit after tax or, more popularly, as the bottom line, permits common shareholder funds to ride free—there is no charge for common equity. Accounting theorists justify this by suggesting that all net profit is attributable to shareholders and they alone as owners can ascertain what is a necessary or required return.

Of course, the critical issue is the kind of behavior that is likely to result, especially if the performance measure is used to evaluate new investment opportunities, including mergers and acquisitions, or for motivating management through incentive compensation. If the charge for capital is too small, what is the likelihood that managers pay too much for new investments? The same is true for incentives. Charge too little for the use of capital and there is no incentive to economize on its use.

One part of the EVA story is the problem of calculating the required return to include all sources of capital. At least as important is getting the calculation of the operating return right. On this score, the accounting framework is a disaster. Stern Stewart numbers more than 120 potential distortions in generally accepted accounting principles, or GAAP. To be pleasant, we call them accounting anomalies. Unless managers fix this problem, EVA is useless as a management process.

It is my belief that one reason for EVA's popularity is its conversion of accounting information to economic reality that can be readily understood by nonfinancial managers. In almost every EVA training program conducted on behalf of our clients, we hear participants—typically operating managers—who can barely read or understand audited financial statements comment about EVA as a performance measure, "Now, this really makes sense!"

Left alone, GAAP distorts economic reality and leads to resource misallocation within the firm. Imagine the consequences of incentive programs that reinforce GAAP measures, such as the bottom line, that can easily encourage shareholder wealth destruction. What would you do if up to 50% of your total compensation was an incentive tied to the growth in annual net earnings and you detected a deteriorating profit margin? Would you be tempted to cut back on research and development (R&D), advertising, or other items that GAAP treats as costs, but that EVA capitalizes, to ensure your own incentive payments?

One of the principal purposes of this book is to present actual case illustrations of the EVA framework's solutions to accounting anomalies and to demonstrate how we align shareholder and management interests to make them congruent. Thus, EVA is a performance measure, but just as important, it is the basis for incentives that drive behavior. EVA *requires* incentives to drive desired outcomes. We believe that without the incentives, EVA becomes just another measure; without incentives, there can be no sustained change in behavior.

An attendant issue in the development of EVA, a question we have been asked often, is, why now? Why, after more than 200 years? The answer can be found in a profound evolution in financial economics that began only 40 years ago. The story begins with published research of Nobel laureates Merton H. Miller (the University of Chicago) and Franco Modigliani (MIT) in 1958, 1960, and 1961. For the first time, the basic theory of microeconomics was applied to corporate finance and showed why the economic model of the firm, not the accounting framework, was to be preferred. In short, they showed that:

- The key driver of value is economic income and a required rate of return directly proportional to risk.
- A firm's market value is the result of rational behavior at the margin by what I call lead steer investors who dominate the process of expectations in setting share prices.
- Capital structure risk can be discerned independently of a firm's asset or business risk.

In its simplest terms, the Miller-Modigliani framework showed us why discounted cash flow as a process and net present value as a measure reflect how markets work in the real world, and thus comprise the approach managers should employ if they are concerned with the impact of their decisions on shareholder value. As a result, DCF and NPV became a practical methodology. Discounted cash flow is a process for placing value on the timing of the receipt and disbursement of cash benefits and costs when investment decisions are evaluated; DCF contains a time value for money so that near-term receipts and disbursements are more significant that more distant cash flows. Net present value, in contrast, uses a specific interest rate for the time value of money that reflects the underlying riskiness attached to receiving benefits or incurring expenditures. I refer to this as the required rate on return for risk. In the literature of corporate finance, it is referred to as the cost of capital.

But not so fast. While the premier business schools graduated more than 100,000 MBAs between 1958 and 1991, the senior management of firms still clung to accounting measures, especially for incentives. Something was wrong, and it was not just the performance measure. So-called conglomerates became all the rage. Diversification was in; homogeneous, single-industry firms were out. Highly successful firms, including Coca-Cola, experimented in unrelated activities with poor results. Where value synergies did occur, a competitive market for potential sellers eliminated the benefits for the buyer. On average, the best the buyer generated was zero EVA on conglomerate-type investments. Usually, shareholders suffered significant wealth destruction.

In retrospect, the conglomeration of firms represented redundant diversification. The lead steers, who set the share prices, already held well-diversified portfolios, and they did not need to have the corporations whose shares they purchased engage in diversification for them a second time. Furthermore, the lead steers acquired their portfolios at existing market prices. Conglomerates, in contrast, paid premiums by acquiring control of their investments. Clearly, something was wrong with the governance systems of such firms. Put another way, the premiums paid by conglomerates to acquire diversification were equivalent to charitable contributions made to random passersby. These premiums represented true corporate waste, and within a reasonably short time the lead steers sent this message in exclamation points to those managements by driving down their share prices to reflect overpayments. In these instances, corporate governance had failed.

Instead of using net present value to evaluate projects, senior management and boards of directors retained the accounting framework by focusing on earnings per share. We all remember those days when firms that commanded high price-to-earnings ratios supposedly could purchase firms with lower P/Es because in an equity exchange the buyer's EPS increased. But the reverse transaction was anathema in the boardroom because it lowered earnings per share. This was the height of naïveté, since the combined firms were exactly the same no matter who did the acquiring. It was at this time in corporate history that the use of net present value and discounted cash flow reached widespread rejection, which puzzled finance professors, whose research indicated that EPS manipulations were nonsense.

Why did companies universally reject NPV? The problem with NPV is that it is a stock measure, whereas annual incentives must be based on a flow measure. That is, the reason for the rejection of NPV as a measure that discounts cash flow was that it could not be used as an incentive device for senior management. As you will see in Chapter 5, EVA and NPV give identical answers in valuing companies. However, because EVA is a flow measure, it can be used as a device for period-by-period contemporaneous incentive compensation.

In summary, the Miller-Modigliani papers were largely responsible for validating the economic model of the firm and NPV as a general description of value on a decision-by-decision basis. They provided a basis for the development of EVA as a workable solution to performance measurement and incentive compensation that makes management behavior and shareholder needs congruent. But shareholders need managers to focus on sustainable improvements in EVA. Thus, incentives require the use of a deferred account that is at risk, and subject to loss, if annual improvement in EVA is not sustained over time. This is a crucial element in making lead steers strong supporters of the EVA concept. To the lead steers, incentives are only a method for developing proper corporate governance. In order to make managers act like owners, the key is not shares or legal title, but rather monies held at risk that are lost if improvements in performance are not sustained.

The second step of the post-1958 revolution was the publication in

1975 of a seminal paper on agency theory by professors William Meckling (the University of Rochester) and Michael Jensen (Harvard Business School). Their major thrust was that managers could be expected to suborn shareholder interests for their own agenda and that shareholders and lenders would have to incur monitoring costs to hold management accountable. In the absence of some kind of police action to control management, firms would squander large amounts of potential shareholder value, but the situation was made worse still by the leftist political economic climate in the 1970s that encouraged members of boards of directors to follow an *independent* line; that is, independent of shareholder concerns and in favor of other constituencies, including suppliers, labor, the community, and the environment. At least as harmful, directors encouraged management to increase market share and to achieve growth for its own sake, even if shareholder value was sacrificed, often with disastrous results.

In 1986, a paper by Jensen on "The Agency Costs of Free Cash Flow" explained how under existing corporate structure so-called free cash flow (i.e., funds not necessary to maintain a firm's existing asset structure and return) was used to cross-subsidize low-returning projects, especially in unrelated activities. And in his 1989 *Harvard Business Review* article entitled "The Eclipse of the Public Corporation," he explained why publicly traded firms would disappear into Kohlberg Kravis Roberts–type structures that more closely aligned ownership and manager interests. KKR is an agent organization and, like many others, selects transactions to be consummated, while arranging financing and providing a significant equity infusion to control the ownership stake in the transaction. Typically, they ask the managers who operate the investments to provide their own equity infusion as well for a small minority ownership position. Normally, the operating managers invest a significant part of their own personal wealth, so their interests and those of the agent firm are very aligned.

Thus, the ultimate police action began with unfriendly takeovers (or the threat of unfriendly takeovers) and leveraged buyouts that would, at long last, rescue shareholders from wasteful investments and poorly focused managers and boards of directors.

In retrospect, Michael Jensen's theories have had a pronounced impact on EVA. For Jensen, the KKR format was a highly successful innovation: huge amounts of debt for a leveraged buyout, with managers then narrowly focused on debt repayment, perhaps with repeated leveraged recapitalizations to maintain their focus well into the future. Jensen's concern was principally with firms that might be described as players in mature industries. I suppose he meant basic industries such as steel, cement, paper, and automobiles, where, at best, new investment could be expected to return a zero EVA—a return equal only to the required return for risk.

However, I am not convinced. I believe this role for debt is largely unnecessary or of secondary importance with EVA programs driven by incentive compensation in the form of uncapped variable pay that is tied to sustainable improvements in EVA. The evidence from hundreds of successful implementations clearly demonstrates that firms possess enormous amounts of hidden value, untapped performance that is released when EVA incentives are carried down throughout the organization, even to the shop floor, and make all employees partners in creating sustainable improvements in EVA. This is "employee capitalism" at its finest!

Of course, as assets are jointly used down deep through an organization, and where transfer pricing also becomes difficult to resolve, our recommendation is to use EVA drivers as the focus of incentives. An EVA driver is that piece of the company's performance over which the employees deeper down in an organization have control. Why try to create incentives on the basis of EVA when an EVA driver is all that an employee can really be expected to influence?

I always held the view that if an entire industry appeared dormant, if not dead, it could be reawakened if employees were made partners in creating sustainable improvements in EVA. For example, as soon as automotive parts suppliers SPX, Federal-Mogul, and Echlin adopted EVA, they just as suddenly generated stretch outcomes. One example in the office furniture industry, Herman Miller, is another startling surprise. All of these would have been candidates for Jensen's gigantic debt package to extract current free cash flow because he would have seen these companies, and their industries, as mature.

Unnecessary, I would say, as their new path was designed around EVA incentives down to the shop floor. The average worker became a value change agent. In 28 months, SPX's share price increased more than five times from $15 to $78, and Herman Miller's price quadrupled in less than two years. Today, when firms announce their intention to implement our brand of EVA, we have found that their share price gains as much as 30% in just one week! The most recent example occurred in February 1998 when Omnicare's shares increased from $28 to $39—an $11 per share increase—simply after its announcement that it was joining our EVA family.

The market is so convinced of the commitment of SPX's chief executive officer, John B. Blystone, to EVA (even his share options have the equivalent of a rising exercise price—no plain vanilla options for him) that the firm was able to eliminate its dividend in 1997 without a whimper from its shareholders. They know he will undertake only projects with positive expected EVA.

This is the message in this volume. Average employees can become value change agents if existing disincentives that smother hidden value are replaced by an EVA program that is carried down throughout the organization. Then EVA improvement is rewarded in individual EVA centers where employees can influence the outcome. It is noteworthy that at Briggs & Stratton (another mature company), Centura Banks, and Harnischfeger Industries employees no longer recommend projects that are EVA-negative because their variable pay tied to EVA improvements eliminates the temptation to score on the basis of size.

This, too, is part of the EVA psychology. In a world where EVA has not yet been implemented, all employees suffer from a common problem. On average, their fixed pay—salary plus pension—is too large, and their variable pay—profit sharing plus shares and/or share options—is too low. Another problem is that their incentive pay is capped. Their rational response to traditional compensation necessarily leads them to go for size. The reason is that size and fixed compensation are closely linked, and that even with capped variable pay, the variable component can be made uncapped by increases in size. That is, increases in size lead to increases in fixed pay, and variable pay follows closely thereafter. Thus, the rational response of employees to traditional compensation methods is to go for size, even if it destroys shareholder value, because increases in size increase both their fixed pay and their variable pay, even if the variable pay is capped in relation to fixed pay.

In contrast, EVA removes the cap on pay, but protects shareholder interests by depositing the variable pay into a deferred account that can be lost if the gains that created the variable pay are not sustained. It is the at-risk nature of variable pay that makes employees truly sensitive to shareholder needs.

The brand of EVA we have trademarked is different, and not just in terms of definition and measure, but in the dynamic behavior change that makes all constituencies participants in shareholder wealth creation. How do we know? Because even people in government or other nonprofit organizations, or in public utilities where a culture of value maximization had been dormant, are now the envy of private sector firms. The United States Postal Service is a particularly noteworthy example. The USPS's Postmaster General, Marvin Runyon, deserves a special commendation for making the effort to convert an inefficient and wasteful organization into a champion of EVA value maximization, an outstanding achievement in a remarkable career. I salute him and all the other hundreds of chief executives who have decided that EVA is the tool of choice in converting employees into value change agents. Their employees feel better about themselves and the role they play as they make employee capitalism an example for others to follow.

EVA

1

The EVA Revolution

This book celebrates a revolution in management known as EVA. With all the attention it has gotten in the press, most executives have heard something about EVA by now. *FORTUNE* magazine has called it "today's hottest financial idea and getting hotter," and management guru Peter Drucker, writing in the *Harvard Business Review*, has described EVA as a vital measure of total factor productivity, one that reflects all the dimensions by which management can increase value. Still, we suspect that most executives, even those inside the finance department, still have only a vague notion of what EVA is and what it can do for their company. We hope to correct that by showing, with an absolute minimum of equations and financial jargon, that EVA truly is, to quote *FORTUNE* again, "the real key to creating wealth."

At its most basic, EVA, an acronym for *economic value added*, is a measure of corporate performance that differs from most others by including a charge against profit for the cost of all the capital a company employs. But EVA is much more than just a measure of performance. It is the framework for a complete financial management and incentive compensation system that can guide every decision a company makes, from the boardroom to the shop floor; that can transform a corporate culture; that can improve the working lives of everyone in an organization by making them more successful; and that can help them produce greater wealth for shareholders, customers, and themselves.

The capital charge in EVA is what economists call an opportunity cost. It is the return that investors could expect to get by putting their money in a portfolio of other stocks and bonds of comparable risk, and that they forego by owning the securities of the company in question. The capital charge embodies the fundamental precept, dating all the way back to Adam Smith, that a business has to produce a minimum, competitive return on *all* the capital invested in it. This cost of capital, or required rate of return, applies to equity as well as debt. Just as lenders demand their interest payments, shareholders insist on getting at least a minimum acceptable rate of return on the money they have at risk. Viewed another way, EVA is profit the way shareholders measure it. If shareholders expect a minimum return of, say, 12% on their investment, they don't begin to "make money" until profits rise above that.

As Peter Drucker put it in his 1995 *Harvard Business Review* article: "EVA is based on something we have known for a long time: What we call profits, the money left to service equity, is usually not profit at all. Until a business returns a profit that is greater than its cost of capital, it operates at a loss. Never mind that it pays taxes as if it had a genuine profit. The enterprise still returns less to the economy than it devours in resources. . . . Until then it does not create wealth; it destroys it." Many corporate managers have forgotten this basic principle because they have been conditioned to focus on conventional accounting profits, which include a deduction for interest payments on debt but have no provision at all for the cost of equity capital. Worse still, most line managers focus on operating profits, which don't even have a charge for debt. True profits don't begin until the cost of capital, like all other costs, has been covered.

EVA is a measure of those true profits. Arithmetically, it is after-tax operating profits minus the appropriate capital charge for both debt and equity. What remains is the dollar amount by which profits in any given period exceed or fall short of the cost of all capital used to produce those profits. This is a number that economists refer to as residual income, which means exactly what it implies: It is the residue left over after *all* costs have been covered. Economists also refer to this as economic profit or economic rent. We call it EVA, for economic value added. It's that simple, though the actual calculation of EVA is somewhat more complicated. It first requires a number of decisions (which will be discussed in detail later on) about how to properly measure operating profits, how to measure capital, and how to determine the cost of capital. Here's the formula:

$$EVA = NOPAT - C\%(TC)$$

where NOPAT is net operating profits after taxes, C% is the percentage cost of capital, and TC is total capital.

This simple formula is the foundation for a revolution in management. "Revolution" is a horridly overused word, of course, routinely summoned into service to pump up management fads that barely qualify as mild disturbances. But we are confident that you will come to agree that EVA is a bona fide revolution, one that can help any corporation, public or private, in any industry, produce superior results for shareholders, employees, and customers. The EVA revolution already is well under way. More than 300 companies on every continent (except Antarctica, of course), with revenues approaching a trillion dollars a year, have implemented Stern Stewart's EVA framework for financial management and incentive compensation. EVA, in turn, has helped the managers of these companies create hundreds of billions of dollars in shareholder wealth that wouldn't otherwise exist.

The Coca-Cola Company, for example, had long been No. 1 in soft drinks but it was decidedly mediocre in the wealth creation department in 1983 when the late Roberto Goizueta became one of the first chief executive officers to adopt EVA. Yet by 1994 Coke had become the No. 1 wealth creator in the world, and by the end of 1996 its sugar water had enriched shareholders by $125 billion. As CEO, Goizueta plainly deserves the credit for Coke's stupendous performance, but EVA played an important role. "We are very pleased to have been one of the first on board the EVA wagon," Goizueta said in 1995. "EVA has given our people a very useful tool for running their individual business units and a sound principle to guide their daily behavior."

The stocks of more recent converts—Eli Lilly, Monsanto, Briggs & Stratton, and Herman Miller, to name a few—have been exceptionally strong performers since those corporations made the switch to EVA, far outpacing the overall market and other companies in their industries. SPX Corporation, a faltering auto parts company in Muskegon, Michigan, implemented EVA in 1996, and its stock price shot from the mid teens to $69 a share in just two years; the company created nearly $350 million of shareholder wealth in its first year on EVA and another $400 million in the second year. SPX workers, so recently demoralized, have become proud, charged-up members of a winning team. EVA is helping reshape South African business as that country moves out from under the stifling blanket of trade embargoes and relearns how to compete in the global market. New Zealand is using EVA to invigorate its state-owned enterprises. Even the United States Postal Service is using EVA to improve efficiency and service and to motivate the largest civilian labor force in the world.

EVA also has gained broad acceptance in the academic community and the business press, and it is changing the way Wall Street picks stocks. Some of the Street's most prominent firms, including Goldman Sachs and Credit Suisse First Boston, have formally adopted EVA as a principal tool for valuing companies, and many others in the United States, Europe, Asia, and Latin America are following their lead. Major institutional investors are turning to EVA as well. Oppenheimer Capital, a pension and mutual fund manager with an exceptionally good track record, has a special affinity for EVA companies. And the California Public Employee Retirement System (CalPERS), the leader in the shareholder activism movement, is now using *poor* EVA performance to identify the list of "focus" companies it selects each year as those most in need of governance reform. Says Bob Boldt, a senior investment officer at CalPERS: "It's simple enough to apply consistently to all companies but complex enough to be useful in showing real economic returns."

EVA resonates with so many constituencies because it entails much more than a fleeting emphasis on a single aspect of corporate performance. Rather, EVA is a return to basics, a rediscovery of the most fundamental elements of business management that brings a lasting change in a company's priorities, systems, and culture. EVA has been proven to work virtually everywhere because it is the right approach for all companies in all times and in all environments.

Like so many revolutionary innovations, this simple tool can be put to extraordinary use. At heart, it is the practical application of both modern financial theory and classical economics to the problems of running a business, an application that turns out to provide the most effective framework for corporate decision making in a period of remarkable economic change. In some ways, it's no surprise that EVA, which attunes managers to the discipline of markets by focusing them on capital costs, has come to the fore in an era when the world has been won over to free enterprise, and markets rule. What EVA is *not* is another form of rightsizing or downsizing or the financial version of reengineering. Nor is it a fad. EVA is a fundamental way of measuring and managing corporate performance that has roots as old as capitalism itself. It tells managers to do those things that they intuitively know are the right things to do, but that so often are obscured by conventional accounting-based measures of performance.

When companies employ EVA to the fullest, which is what they must do to change behavior, it becomes far more than just another way of adding up costs and computing profits. It is:

- The corporate performance measure that is tied most directly, both theoretically and empirically, to the creation of shareholder wealth; as you will see, managing for higher EVA is, by definition, managing for a higher stock price.
- The only performance measure that always gives the "right" answer, in the sense that more EVA always is unambiguously better for shareholders, which makes it the only genuine continuous-improvement metric; in contrast, actions that increase profit margins, earnings per share, and even rates of return sometimes destroy shareholder wealth.
- The framework underlying a comprehensive new system of corporate financial management that guides every decision, from annual operating budgets to capital budgeting, strategic planning, and acquisitions and divestitures.
- A simple but effective method for teaching business literacy to even the least sophisticated workers.
- The key variable in a unique incentive compensation system that, for the first time, truly aligns the interests of managers with those of shareholders and causes managers to think like and act like owners.
- A framework that companies can use to communicate their goals and achievements to investors, and that investors can use to identify companies with superior performance prospects—what Steve Einhorn, director of global equity research at Goldman Sachs, calls "a power tool in the analyst's tool kit."
- Most important, an internal system of corporate governance that motivates all managers and employees to work cooperatively and enthusiastically to achieve the very best performance possible.

The financial management system—the set of financial policies and procedures, and measures and methods, that guide and control a company's operations and strategy—concerns such things as setting and communicating financial goals, both internally and externally; evaluating both short-term profit plans and long-term strategic plans; allocating resources, from deciding whether to buy a new piece of equipment to acquiring and divesting entire companies; evaluating operating performance from a financial perspective; and tracing the sources of that performance back to the strategic and operating levers available to managers.

Those are things that all companies must do, but our experience is that most companies do them badly. Indeed, the typical financial management system today isn't a system at all. Rather, it's a hodgepodge of rules, guidelines, and procedures that employs an array of frequently contradictory measures and objectives, that fosters confusion and conflict within an organization, that focuses on performance variables that bear little relation to the value of a business, and that often leads smart managers to do dumb things. Companies may evaluate individual products or lines of business on the basis of operating profits. Business units may be evaluated in terms of return on assets or a budgeted profit figure. Finance departments analyze capital investments in terms of discounted cash flow, but evaluate acquisitions by the effect on earnings growth. EVA, in contrast, provides a single, consistent focus, and allows all decisions to be modeled, monitored, communicated, and evaluated in exactly the same terms—the incremental wealth that a particular course of action will create or destroy.

The EVA framework provides a new lens through which managers view a corporation, a lens that gives a clearer perception of the underlying economics of a business and enables any manager to make better decisions. The capital charge, for example, causes managers throughout a company to consider the effects that their decisions have on the balance sheet as well as the income statement, and gives them a clear, objective basis for weighing trade-offs between the two. Suddenly, production managers begin optimizing the trade-off between long production runs that boost operating profits by reducing unit costs and the higher inventories (and capital costs) that long runs require. Salespeople learn that the generous payment terms they grant in order to land a big order can actually suck all the economic profit out of a sale. As you will see from examples later on, it is hard to overstate the impact that capital awareness can have on the true bottom line and on the ability of an organization to learn and improve in ways that build real competitive advantage.

The EVA system enables managers to make better decisions by providing them with superior information and insights. But information alone won't cause managers to choose the actions that maximize economic profits and shareholder wealth, especially when those actions are difficult or unpleasant. The real magic in EVA comes from changing behavior throughout an organization, and that depends crucially on using it as the basis for incentive compensation. Indeed, if all a company intends to do is measure EVA and use it as one more benchmark of performance, it probably isn't worth the bother. Merely measuring and monitoring EVA is akin to a New Yorker checking the temperature in Honolulu in February: It may be interesting information, but it doesn't affect how you dress.

Many operating managers are gifted with great ingenuity, and all of them have an intense desire to succeed. A central question faced by all top managers and boards of directors is how to harness that ingenuity and desire and direct it in ways that maximize the success of both the individual and the enterprise. The answer lies in human nature: People do what you reward them for doing, not what you exhort them to do. Base incentives on higher operating margins, and you will get higher operating margins, even if it means that sales fall off a cliff. Pay for sales increases, and you'll get more sales; pay for market share, and you'll get market share. The secondary goals and initiatives sent down from the executive suite may get some attention, but a manager or worker's real energy will be focused on the variable that drives his or her bonus or is most likely to lead to a promotion. Thus, if you pay people for generating more EVA, you will get more EVA and, with it, a higher share price and greater shareholder wealth. You also will get a more successful organization that provides greater nonmonetary satisfaction as well.

However—and this is a big however—simply plugging EVA into a conventional, run-of-the-boardroom incentive scheme won't get you anywhere near the performance gains that most organizations are capable of achieving. In fact, the modal incentive compensation system in use today actually is a *dis*incentive system. If you properly analyze the way incentives affect behavior, which we do in Chapter 7, you find that the typical bonus scheme places far too much emphasis on the short term, provides little or no motivation for superior performance, causes managers to be excessively conservative, and encourages them to sit on their hands in boom times and bad times. In short, most incentive schemes drive companies to underperform their potential. They also tend to pay too much for mediocrity and way, way too little for outstanding performance.

We prefer a type of incentive plan that differs radically from the norm. The most important difference is that EVA bonus plans work: They give managers the same visceral identification that an owner has with the success or failure of an enterprise. EVA bonus plans make managers think like and act like owners by paying them like owners. We do that by calculating cash bonuses as a fixed percentage of increases in EVA—in other words, by giving managers a piece of the EVA action. EVA bonus plans also violate two cardinal rules laid down by the big compensation consulting firms. Rule breaker No. 1 is that these bonuses don't have any caps. The more EVA increases, the bigger the bonus—without limits. We are able to do away with upper limits because we pay only for sustainable increases in EVA. A portion of any exceptional bonus award goes into a "bonus bank" for payment in future years, and is forfeited if EVA subsequently falls. Rule breaker No. 2 is that the targets for EVA improvement under the bonus plan are automatically reset by formula instead of negotiating a budgeted level of improvement each year.

The rule breakers are key to the efficacy of EVA incentive plans, which in turn are the heart of the EVA governance system. Doing away with the conventional bonus cap gives a manager a pecuniary reason to continue striving for better and better performance even in boom years. Under conventional incentive plans, in contrast, managers have every reason to go into the leisure mode once their bonuses have "capped out," and to engage in wealth-destroying behavior such as pushing additional sales into the next bonus year. The bonus bank, meanwhile, guards against the temptation to game the system by sacrificing the future for short-term gain. It also gives managers a reason to work long hours to minimize the carnage in a business downturn. Having money at risk in the bonus bank is what turns managers into genuine owners and causes them to lengthen their horizons, constantly seeking out new sources of sustainable, long-term improvement. Similarly, the automatic reset feature spurs performance by decoupling bonuses from annual budgets. Managers with conventional incentive schemes typically try to negotiate modest, easily achievable profit plans in order to be sure of collecting their bonuses. Managers under an EVA bonus plan are encouraged to propose aggressive budgets because they won't be penalized for falling short, and they will get paid extra for everything they do achieve. They swing for the fences instead of settling for singles.

Stock market professionals have begun to pick up on the value that EVA incentives help create. Tony Kreisel of Putnam Investments Management and Andy Pilara of the Robertson Stephens money management firm have a decided preference for companies with EVA bonus plans. So, too, does Eugene Vesell, a senior portfolio manager at Oppenheimer Capital. "We look for managements whose philosophy focuses on the intelligent use of capital as measured by EVA," says Vesell. "We want managements who are incentivized on an EVA basis to produce long-term returns well above their cost of capital." Some securities analysts look on the adoption of an EVA bonus plan as a "buy" indication. When Andrew Cash of PaineWebber raised his recommendation on Olin Corporation from neutral to buy in August 1995, his key message was, "EVA and new compensation system to the rescue." He wrote: "Starting in 1996 management will have 80% or more of their bonus compensation tied to EVA goals. No economic profit through a cycle, no bonus!" Cash's recommendation and a similar one by Leslie Ravitz of Morgan Stanley helped lift Olin stock from $52 to $76 a share in just four months.

Some essential elements in the governance aspect of EVA should be apparent by now. The EVA financial management system shows managers which decisions will increase economic profits and generate the most wealth for shareholders. The bonus system acts as the owner's control mechanism by ensuring that it is in the manager's self-interest to pursue the shareholder's interest. At the same time, the bonus system puts the manager's wealth at risk and penalizes him or her for failing to produce a minimum required rate of return. In essence, this is pay for results, not pay for performance. As Bennett Stewart, the senior partner of Stern Stewart, is fond of saying, "EVA makes managers rich, but only if they make shareholders filthy rich."

At heart, EVA isn't about finance or economics, it's about people. The most valuable resource in any company is the creativity and the will to succeed that all people possess, and usually to a much greater degree than they get credit for. EVA is a means to unlock the potential for achievement that exists throughout every organization. No magic formula handed down by top management or the finance department can accomplish that. But a management system that provides employees with better information and insights, that makes them accountable for performance, and that properly rewards them for success can produce remarkable results. Adopting EVA doesn't magically transform managers into latter-day Hyperboreans who automatically enjoy rising profits through every economic climate. Creating wealth still requires great ingenuity and tireless effort, but those who are equipped with better information and better motivation are far more likely to succeed.

As you undoubtedly have gleaned by now, the EVA system is founded on the proposition that the primary responsibility of management is to maximize shareholder wealth by getting the stock price as high as possible. This view is somewhat controversial, to say the least. Even in the United States, the apogee of free-market economics, many people argue that the single-minded pursuit of shareholder wealth, however it may be measured, is too narrow and coldhearted. Even some corporate chieftains—and many others who ought to know better—argue that such an approach is socially and economically irresponsible because it ignores important and deserving *stakeholders*, including employees, customers, the communities where companies operate, the environment, and even the long-term interests of shareholders themselves. In fact, maximizing shareholder wealth is the best way—indeed, the only way—to effectively serve the long-term interests of all stakeholders. It is the only policy that is genuinely fair to workers. (It also is the only way chief executives can be confident of keeping their jobs in today's environment.)

Few would argue that the proverbial corner grocer should do anything other than run the store to make as much money as possible. But the issue becomes murkier when we move from the owner-operator of a small enterprise (or even a large one) to the professional managers of major corporations with millions of far-flung shareholders. In the stakeholder view of things, shareholders have become so disperse, and their ownership of shares often so fleeting, that they have forfeited their primacy. Simply holding shares doesn't qualify as ownership in the full sense of the word, they say. This is particularly true when the shareholder is further separated from the company by an institutional portfolio manager whose only concern may be to beat the market this quarter in order to buy a Porsche Turbo or, if the manager picks stocks really well, a McLaren F1. Stakeholder advocates maintain that the true responsibility of boards of directors is to balance the claims of competing constituencies, forsaking shareholders whenever their interests unduly infringe on those of employees, the community, or some other deserving group.

Many CEOs are drawn instinctively to the stakeholder philosophy. It is the one most consistent with the parochial conception of the corporation as a quasi-organic entity with a life of its own. This attitude characterized U.S. management in the decades following World War II, and still dominates in much of Europe and Asia today. As Gordon Donaldson of the Harvard Business School observes in

Corporate Restructuring: Managing the Change Process from Within: "In the late Sixties and most of the Seventies, the typical mind-set of top management can be described as follows: an introverted, corporate-centered view of the business mission focused on growth, diversification, and opportunity for the 'corporate family.' In the corporate rhetoric of that period, reference to the stockholder interest was strangely absent, and there was often even a renunciation of 'purely economic' goals."

And what if, as the Donaldson quote implies, the pursuit of growth and diversification for their own sake happened to be hazardous to shareholder wealth? No problem. In those days most corporate boards were Greek choruses that routinely ratified whatever a CEO wanted to do. They replaced CEOs only with the most extreme provocation, such as RCA chief Edgar Griffiths' bizarre failure to file personal income-tax returns for several years. And if stockholders were disappointed in a company's performance, they politely sold their shares and moved on to another investment in what used to be known as "the Wall Street walk." Institutional investors rarely raised objections to corporate actions, and were ignored when they did. Managers also were largely immune to the threat of a takeover. The unfriendly tender offer was the corporate equivalent of mustard gas, and anyone with the audacity to use it was promptly ostracized from the community of respectable executives.

But just as nature abhors a vacuum, markets won't tolerate wasted resources and unexploited opportunities indefinitely. By the late 1970s a profusion of poorly performing companies brought forth a new class of corporate raiders, and Wall Street found ways to finance them. Suddenly, it seemed that everyone was using mustard gas. Even AT&T and American Express, two corporations that once had the whitest shoes on the *FORTUNE* 500, made hostile bids for other companies (American Express muffed its play for McGraw-Hill; AT&T, to its regret, succeeded in overpaying for NCR Corporation). Soon after corporate raiders put the fear of tender offers in the hearts of underperforming managers, a cadre of institutional investors began waving the flag of ownership and banging on boardroom doors. The institutions—the owners—were about as welcome as an Environmental Protection Agency inspector. As late as 1991, 10 of the 12 companies on CalPERS's list of egregious underperformers refused even to meet with the fund's representatives.

Unsurprisingly, the managerial establishment railed against what the press called the takeover wars and the academics dryly termed the "market for corporate control." A disdain for shareholders comes through loudly in a 1990 report on corporate governance by the Business Roundtable (the club made up of CEOs of the 200 largest corporations in the United States): "Shareholder voting on such things as acquisitions and divestitures can put immediate shareholder financial return ahead of sound longer-term growth which may have the potential of being even more rewarding to the corporation, its shareholders *and its other stakeholders*" (emphasis added).

The Roundtable could have taken its text from Time Inc.'s acquisition of Warner Communications the year before. The Time-Warner deal represented the most egregious instance of stakeholder pleading ever, at least in terms of the shareholder wealth sacrificed. While the Time-Warner deal was pending, Martin Davis of Paramount Communications intervened with an offer of $180 a share for Time, which had been trading around $135. Davis subsequently raised his offer to $200, but Time's board asked the Delaware court to prevent Time shareholders from taking it. Time argued that its heritage of journalistic integrity is a "sacred trust," and that a takeover by the Philistines at Paramount might do unconscionable harm to the readers of *Time*, *People*, and *Southern Living*.

The Delaware Chancery Court blocked Davis's tender offer, depriving Time shareholders of a $6.5-billion premium over what their shares were worth before Davis entered the fray. It then took Time Warner Inc. stock *eight years* to rise to the price Davis had offered. The rate of return (including dividends) on Time stock over the period was less than one-third that of the Standard & Poor's 500 index—5.1% versus 16.6%. So, after preventing shareholders from getting a premium, the Time board presided over a lousy investment as well. If one measures the total shareholder loss as what Time's owners would have had by July 1997 if they had been able to take Davis's offer and had reinvested the entire proceeds in an S&P index fund, the court decision cost them $56 billion. *People*'s readers owe a much greater debt to the shareholders than they realize.

All companies fail to maximize shareholder returns to some degree. Try to name a single one that does everything super-efficiently all the time and has no executive perks that aren't absolutely essential to the enterprise. But the pressure to perform has become much more intense in recent years. Today's CEOs know that if they fail in a big way, whether from malfeasance, misfeasance, or nonfeasance, they're out. Even if no raiders come calling, those pesky institutions will see to it, and the CEO's newly fickle friends on the board will go along with them. Just ask John Akers of IBM, Robert Stempel of General Motors, Jimmy Robinson of American Express, Paul Lego of Westinghouse, or any of a host of other displaced chief executives. Hence all the corporate trumpeting of shareholder value initiatives. As any reader of annual reports knows, the mantra of "managing for shareholder value" has become a sine qua non of corporate political correctness. Most companies still are in the dark about exactly how they're supposed to go about managing for shareholder value, but virtually all of them say they are doing it.

After two decades in which corporate raiders have, for the most part, put wasted assets to better use, even the Business Roundtable has finally got the objective right. In a remarkable statement on corporate governance that was crafted under the leadership of Chase Manhattan CEO Walter Shipley in 1997, the Roundtable took the position that "the principle objective of a business enterprise is to generate economic returns to its owners." It went on to say, "The notion that the board must somehow balance the interests of stockholders against the interests of other stakeholders fundamentally misconstrues the role of directors. It is, moreover, an unworkable notion because it would leave the board with no criterion for resolving conflicts between interests of stockholders and of other stakeholders or among different groups of stakeholders."

Why should managers and directors put shareholders ahead of all others? The most obvious reason is that they own the place, but there are more compelling, though less obvious, reasons to maximize shareholder wealth that have little to do with this "finance view" of the corporation. These reasons are founded instead on pure pragmatism. The simple fact is that in a market economy, everyone fares best in the long run when management puts shareholders first.

First and foremost, maximizing shareholder wealth is the action that takes Adam Smith's invisible hand out of its pocket and puts it to work guiding resources to their most productive and highly valued uses. Business, after all, is the greatest engine of wealth in society, and the process of creating shareholder wealth is the same process that creates greater wealth for everyone in an economy. Indeed, creating wealth is the only real source of social security. If companies do not pursue the maximum shareholder wealth possible, resources are squandered and society is poorer. Paradoxically, it is only because we care about maximizing the wealth available for everyone that we should care about maximizing the wealth of shareholders at all. Improving the commonweal is the real reason why maximizing shareholder wealth is so important, and it is the reason why the overriding purpose of corporate governance ought to be to ensure that this rule is followed.

What's more, managers simply cannot create enduring shareholder wealth by abusing other stakeholders. That is because a corporation is nothing more, or less, than what economist Ronald Coase called a nexus of contracts. Written or implied, explicit or merely understood, these contracts are covenants between the company and its stakeholders. Labor, management, and suppliers come together voluntarily and use capital put up by investors to create a product that they hope customers will buy. If management deals shabbily with any constituency—if it violates the contract—the victim will simply stop volunteering. If a company tries to pay wages that are too low, it won't be able to hire the quality of workers it wants and needs. If it pays suppliers too slowly, they will raise prices or demand payment on delivery. If its products fall short of the quality it promises, customers will turn to the competition.

As the Roundtable put the matter in its 1997 statement: "To manage the corporation in the long-term interests of the stockholders, management and the board of directors must take into account the interests of the corporation's other stakeholders." That is due in no small part to the fact that shareholders are the ones who get paid last, only after a company has paid its employees, paid its suppliers, paid its lenders, and paid its taxes. Smart managers understand that the surest way to provide handsome returns to shareholders is to treat all stakeholders well. Not all managers are smart, of course, and some do try to take advantage of one constituency or another. But the long-term costs from a tarnished reputation almost always outweigh any short-run benefits.

It is more than coincidental that research by Curtis C. Verschoor, a professor of accounting at DePaul University, has found a highly significant relationship between financial performance and a corporate commitment to ethical behavior. Verschoor divided 296 large companies into three groups—those that make no commitment in their annual reports to a code of ethics or conduct, those that make some commitment, and those that make a strong commitment. He then compared the market value added, or MVA, of the companies. (MVA is a measure of shareholder wealth creation that is explained in Chapter 3.) Verschoor found that the companies that stressed a strong commitment to ethics had an average MVA of $16.8 billion, versus an average MVA of $11.1 billion for those with some commitment and $5.7 billion for those with no mention of ethics. As John Shiely, president of Briggs & Stratton, puts the matter: "Value-creating companies recognize the importance of ethical behavior."

Top managers and directors have another pragmatic reason to put shareholders first. This one stems from the fact that all corporations, regardless of what they produce or where they produce it, have to compete for a scarce resource called capital. Capital is the medium of exchange that all companies must have to acquire the inputs—labor, materials, technology, and know-how—to produce goods and services to sell to customers. A company's ability to acquire capital at attractive prices depends on how well it performs as a steward of the capital it already has. Those that create shareholder wealth by returning more than the cost of capital will find it easier to raise additional money to invent new products, improve the quality of existing ones, enter new markets, and create more jobs. A company that consistently earns less than the cost of capital, either through ineptitude or by sacrificing shareholder interests to please another stakeholder group, will find that its shares sell at a discount. Additional capital will become increasingly difficult and expensive to come by, the CEO's job will be in jeopardy, the company may become subject to hostile takeover bids, and it ultimately will end up closing plants and offices and firing workers. How quickly these penalties are meted out depends in part on the openness of capital markets and the market for corporate control, but they ultimately are inescapable.

Roberto Goizueta had an uncommon grasp of the overarching importance of creating shareholder wealth. In Coca-Cola's 1993 annual report, Goizueta stated that Coke possessed "a precise focus on why we exist: to create real value for our shareholders over the long term." Expanding on that thought three years later, Goizueta wrote in the 1996 annual report: "Governments are created to help meet civic needs. Philanthropies are created to meet social needs. And companies are created to meet economic needs." Companies that do their job well, he continued, "contribute to society in very meaningful ways." The wealth that Goizueta created certainly contributed meaningfully to Coke's hometown of Atlanta. Shortly after his death in 1997, the *Wall Street Journal* reported just a few of the beneficent things that came about because of the wealth Goizueta created for shareholders:

- Nick Smith, 44, Goizueta's dentist, has a very comfortable nest egg for retirement because he steadily invested in Coke stock ever since he bought his first block of 100 shares in 1984 for $6,237.50, an investment that by itself climbed to a mid-1997 value of $180,000 after four stock splits and reinvested dividends.
- Four local philanthropies that hold Coke stock—the Robert W. Woodruff, Joseph P. Whitehead, Lettie Pate Evans, and Lettie Pate Whitehead foundations—boosted charitable giving from $5 million in 1980 to about $220 million in 1997. Together they have a value of $7.6 billion, almost all from the value of their holdings of 119 million Coke shares.
- One beneficiary of their giving is Trees Atlanta, a group accustomed to planting only about 100 trees a year on an $80,000 annual budget. With the foundations chipping in $2 million, the group planted 15,000 oaks, maples, magnolias, and hollies from 1992 to 1996, sprucing up the city in time for the Olympic Games.
- Emory University has seen its own endowment rise in value from $250 million in 1981 to become one of the nation's largest at $3.8 billion. The university holds about 40 million Coke shares, making up 63% of the value of that endowment. Emory has built facilities, offered scholarships, endowed professorships, and expanded programs that might not have been funded without the gain in its endowment wealth.
- An example of the endowment at work is the Roberto C. Goizueta Business School at Emory. At the dedication ceremony in the summer of 1997, Goizueta's son, Roberto S., a theology student at Loyola, thanked Emory and the audience on behalf of his then ailing father: "Dad believed very strongly that business is the best way to contribute to society—because it is how opportunity is created."

The EVA approach to wealth creation also can be extremely rewarding to workers. Just ask the folks at Herman Miller, the Zeeland, Michigan, furniture maker that is renowned for its Eames lounge chair and other superb designs. Miller is equally famous for its egalitarian style of management. Nearly a half-century ago, the company became one of the first to adopt a Scanlon plan in which all employees share in the profits of the enterprise. Herman Miller prides itself on treating all employees as equals, and was an early leader in the development of participative management and work teams. Yet the management team at Herman Miller has always recognized that wealth creation is essential to success. As Hugh DePree, the son of founder J. J. DePree, wrote in the corporate history, *Business as Unusual*, the philosophy at Herman Miller always emphasized performance and productivity as keys to the well-being of the organization.

Even so, Herman Miller ran into trouble in the mid-1990s. Coming out of a huge slump in the office furniture business, the company's sales were growing faster than the industry's, but the results weren't showing up on the bottom line. "We had effectively lost our way," says chief financial officer (CFO) Brian Walker. "We were throwing all kinds of assets onto the balance sheet that were not productive or we didn't need. We really thought capital was free, and so the business was having a heart attack." That's when top management turned to EVA, which it saw as being particularly well suited to the company's environment of what it calls employee-owners (they all have stock).

The managers were right. In its first full year on the new financial management system, Herman Miller's EVA jumped from $10 million to more than $40 million. "EVA analysis has enabled us to identify waste in both our costs and our use of capital," says CEO Michael A. Volkema. "This has led to the reduction of nonproductive assets such as inventory and accounts receivable." Over the past two years, as sales have risen 38%, Herman Miller employees found ways to cut inventories 24% and reduce the total square footage of building space by more than 15%.

Herman Miller also has cut its receivables days outstanding from 45 in 1992 to just 30 in 1997. But Herman Miller didn't speed up payments because the controller's office ordered the divisions to hector customers. When they went on EVA and began focusing on capital costs like receivables, Miller employees in the divisions attacked the late payment problem on their own and discovered that the cause of overdue receivables was incomplete orders. When an order arrived missing a piece or two, the customer would withhold all payments until the last items arrived. So the Millerites got receivables down by speeding up production of those missing items and making sure shipments were complete as well as on time. The result: improvements in both EVA and customer satisfaction.

The changes have paid off for shareholders, pushing Herman Miller stock from a low of $27 a share in 1995 to a high of $36.25 in the early months of 1998—after a four-for-one stock split. EVA also has profited the Herman Miller workers. "EVA has been a great tool for the people of Herman Miller," says Volkema. "Our people understand it and put it to work every day. EVA builds on our historic strength of employee participation, allowing our employee-owners to better understand the impact of their actions, resulting in better decisions for our customers and our business. We've seen our business grow, but equally important, we've seen our people grow in their commitment and contribution to Herman Miller." Their net worths have grown as well. Volkema estimates that the wealth of Herman Miller employees rose more than $100 million in less than two years on EVA. In the third quarter of fiscal 1997 alone, rank-and-file employees got an EVA bonus payout equal to 31% of wages.

Just as maximizing shareholder wealth enriches everyone, the failure to do so diminishes living standards. Proof of this can been seen in a fascinating 1996 study of international productivity by the McKinsey Global Institute, part of McKinsey & Company. The researchers wanted to solve two riddles: Why is German labor productivity lower than United States productivity even though Germany uses 40% more capital per worker than the United States? And why is per capita output lower in Japan than in the United States when Japan has saved so much more and its people work many more hours per year? The German situation is a paradox because the amount of capital per worker is a key determinant of labor productivity. With 40% more capital per worker, Germany ought to have much higher output per capita despite the fact that its people work only 82% as many hours per year as Americans. The Japanese situation seems even more puzzling. Its people invest more money *and* more time and energy to get back less in return. The researchers concluded that the answers to the two riddles are the same. The reason that both countries have lower output per capita isn't because there is something wrong with German or Japanese workers. The problem is that *capital* productivity in both countries is less than two-thirds the level in the United States. In other words, the problem isn't labor productivity. Rather, it is the efficiency with which managers use the capital they have invested.

Why does this matter? Because higher capital productivity means that American workers are much better off than their German or Japanese counterparts. In comparison with German workers, whose earnings are very close to those in the United States, U.S. workers save less of their incomes and consume more, enjoying a much higher standard of living. Meanwhile, the greater capital productivity gives rise to higher rates of return on investments, so that the savings of American workers grow faster and they wind up with greater financial assets and a better lifestyle in retirement even though they save less. The comparison with Japanese workers is even more favorable. Americans work less, save much less, have a much better lifestyle, and wind up with greater financial assets. That's pretty good, and all because companies are using capital more productively.

But why the difference? The researchers concluded that it is because German and Japanese managers put other priorities ahead of shareholder wealth, and not because of any fundamental differences in the two societies. Concluded McKinsey: "Surprisingly, we found that managers in Japan and Germany could achieve performance close to U.S. levels if they ran their companies differently, which they appear free to do. Formal external constraints, such as labor laws and rules, do not fundamentally restrict improvement opportunities." Part of the problem in Germany is the overengineering and gold-plating of facilities, something that may be peculiar to the German psyche but seems to afflict production managers everywhere. A bigger problem in both countries is the practice of buying domestic goods rather than imports even when the imports are cheaper. The Germans and Japanese take their economic chauvinism much more seriously than Lee Iacocca, who filmed a "Buy American" TV spot wearing a Burberry raincoat. And the Germans and Japanese pay a heavy price for it. The McKinsey researchers estimate that global sourcing of equipment could save German and Japanese companies from 10% in the food industry to as much as 60% in telecommunications.

One of the biggest differences between the United States and other countries, McKinsey observes, is the greater discipline of the stock market: "More so in the U.S. than elsewhere, the capital market boosts productivity because it gives managers a clear primary objective—financial performance—that generally guides them to use their resources productively. Furthermore, the U.S. capital market complements the competitive pressures of the product market by cutting off funds to failing firms. Consequently, the high levels of productivity attained in most U.S. industries do not square with the 'conventional wisdom' that the U.S. capital market undermines economic performance by forcing firms to be too focused on short-term results." Lest you think McKinsey is giving too much credit to the stock market, consider this: The takeover movement began forcing managers to focus more squarely on stock returns in the late seventies and early eighties, and the eighties happen to be the first decade in the postwar era when U.S. competitiveness increased relative to other industrial nations.

While the United States leads the world in productivity and living standards, our experience indicates that most corporations still waste prodigious amounts of capital. Every company Stern Stewart has worked with to implement EVA has discovered deep pockets of capital inefficiency when managers began focusing on the balance sheet as well as the income statement. That's actually very good news, because it means there still is room for enormous immediate gains in wealth creation in the United States. The potential elsewhere, of course, is much greater.

The coming chapters will explain why every company should be using the EVA financial management and incentive compensation systems to measure performance, shape decisions, and motivate employees. We will explain how to measure wealth creation and how to directly compare the performances of companies in different industries, and why managing for higher EVA is the surest way to create wealth. Along the way, we also will describe how some pathbreaking companies already have used EVA to unlock the wealth-creating ingenuity that exists in all enterprises.

2

Revving the Engine at Briggs & Stratton

The antique Flyer in the lobby of Briggs & Stratton's Milwaukee headquarters was something less than a flyaway success. Built in 1920, the Flyer was little more than a sled with a noisy two-horsepower engine sitting atop four wheels. It sold for about $200 at a time when motorists could pick up a brand-new Model T Ford for $350, which probably explains why Briggs sold only two thousand of the curious vehicles. Briggs & Stratton also made a genuine car called the Superior, but the elegant open tourer didn't live up to its name, either. Briggs made just three of them. Steve Briggs and Henry Stratton, who cofounded the company in 1909 as an auto parts supplier, finally began to prosper when they set their sights lower down on the power train, so to speak. In 1919 they acquired the rights to a gadget called the Smith motor wheel, which became the heart of the company's low-horsepower, air-cooled engines. By the thirties they were attaching the engines to just about any kind of home and garden appliance, from washing machines to cultivators to power saws.

Lawn mowers, though, proved to be the real winner for the company. If postwar Americans bought suburban houses like there was no tomorrow, they cut their grass like there was rain tomorrow. The lightweight Briggs & Stratton engine was ideally suited to power mowers, and the company soon came to dominate the booming lawn mower engine business. Briggs burgeoned with suburbia, eventually settling in a 1.5-million-square-foot factory on Burleigh Street in nearby Wauwautosa, Wisconsin. Along the way, the company continued to produce auto parts and also turned out such unlikely offerings as candy stands, coin-operated towel dispensers, and rifle grenades. But inexpensive air-cooled engines were the product that powered the company's prosperity. And Briggs & Stratton did prosper. The company went solidly into the black in 1929 and stayed there for 60 years, through 11 U.S. presidents, three wars, Parcheesi®, and mood rings.

Until 1989, that is, when a decade of competition from Japanese engine makers finally left Briggs & Stratton with a loss of $20 million. "After 60 straight years of making money, a loss for us was countercultural," says company president John Shiely. The deficit was so traumatic that chairman Frederick P. Stratton, Jr. (Henry's grandson) ordered a restructuring that shook the company to its core. The makeover included the sale of one of Briggs's oldest divisions, the reorganization of the company into seven business units, and the relocation of many of its operations. The most important element, however, was the adoption of EVA. "Given the enormous changes we made," says CFO Robert Eldridge, "coming across EVA when we did . . . well, the timing was exquisite."

So were the results. Largely under the leadership of John Shiely, Briggs & Stratton took the EVA framework literally to the shop floor. The company trained most of its rank-and-file workers in the EVA concept that capital costs on the balance sheet are just as important as operating costs on the income statement, and asked each of them to make frequent suggestions of ways to improve the EVA of their particular functions. After a bitter dispute with one union local, the company eventually put all its workers on EVA incentives—even ones in a joint venture in mainland China. The results have been stupendous. Shares of Briggs & Stratton languished in the teens throughout the 1980s while most other stocks bounded upward in the bull market. But most of the time since adopting EVA, Briggs stock has handily outpaced the market, and then some. By 1997 it had hit $53 a share, with a two-for-one split along the way. The gratifying change in relative stock market performance reflects an equally dramatic change in the way those at Briggs & Stratton go about their jobs.

Like many companies, Briggs & Stratton had been preoccupied with accounting profits and largely ignored what was happening to its balance sheet. The company got fat, with too much inventory, too much equipment, and too much manpower. "We had nearly ten thousand employees in the old engine plant on Burleigh Street," says Shiely. "It was a monument to Taylorism. What had been a competitive juggernaut became an albatross." The error of its ways wasn't apparent in the early postwar decades, when Briggs had a virtual lock on the small-engine business. But, by the late 1970s powerful rivals like Honda and Kawasaki had arrived on the scene and threatened to make off with some of Briggs's oldest customers. At the same time, the lawn-and-garden landscape was shifting. Homeowners no longer went to the local John Deere store to buy their mowers. They went to Wal-Mart. And for the Wal-Marts of the world, price was the prime consideration in deciding what line of lawn mowers to carry. "With the mass-marketization of the lawn mower business, the prices of low-end models barely increased," says Shiely. "By the late 1980s, Wal-Mart and Kmart had even stopped giving us inflation increases."

The biggest advantage the Japanese had over Briggs was labor costs, so Briggs responded by trying to automate itself out of its problems. The company threw huge amounts of capital into robotics and other cutting-edge technologies in an attempt to reduce labor costs and preserve operating margins. "We were very poor at capital management," says controller James Brenn. "We could always justify plowing money back into automation." Briggs also persisted in putting out a complete line of air-cooled engines, from the smallest and cheapest to the largest and most powerful, and took pride in making almost all components in-house.

The capital tied up in operations nearly tripled between 1979 and 1989, going from $175 million to $488 million. Accounting profits and cash flow remained fairly steady, but the company's EVA—its true profit after deducting the opportunity cost of that swelling capital base—headed south like it was riding a Flyer. The capital charge (the weighted average cost of capital times the capital invested) shot from $24.4 million in 1979 to $64.7 million in 1989. "In the late seventies," says Shiely, "the ratio of operating capital to net income was three to one. It took us three dollars invested in bricks and mortar and plant and equipment to generate a dollar of net income. By the late eighties, the ratio was nine to one. We were using three times as much capital to generate each dollar of net income." By the time the accounting numbers showed a loss of $20 million in 1989, EVA was down to minus $62 million. "It was like the old Pall Mall ad," says Shiely. "We were smoking more but enjoying it less."

"We weren't good capital managers, and therefore we weren't rewarding our shareholders," says CFO Eldridge. "Fred Stratton was determined to do something to better maximize shareholder value." What Stratton did was take a sledgehammer to the engine block. In July 1989 he announced that the company would refocus on high-volume, low-cost engines and effectively bow out of the premium engine market. In addition, the company was to be broken up into seven stand-alone business units, each turning out a distinct product or product line, and each with its own bottom line.

The manufacturing process in each division would be radically altered, with Japanese-style focus factories and cell manufacturing replacing the traditional batch approach. (In batch processing, similar machines are lined up together, and the operators turn out a single part without regard for the next operation down the line. In cell manufacturing, different types of machines are grouped together and operators and assemblers work as a team, turning out a complete subassembly or even a complete product.) The idea was to skinny down, to shed the "crank-out-the-inventory" approach that had become standard operating procedure at the Burleigh plant. "When I first heard about the focus factories, I didn't think it would work," says Gary Zingler, operations manager at the large engine division in Wauwautosa. "I thought, 'You're going to get rid of inventory? You're nuts.' "

Stratton also had decided to ditch earnings per share as the yardstick for corporate performance. He recognized that EPS did not adequately capture the company's wealth-destroying dependency on capital outlays. "We had accumulated so much cash around the place that our people figured it didn't have a cost," recalls Shiely. What's more, the new structure of the company seemed to cry out for a new performance metric. "We had decided to go ahead with the divisionalization," notes controller Brenn, "and we knew we needed something to accurately measure the performance of those new divisions."

Brenn had been won over to EVA back in 1986 while attending an EVA seminar in Chicago. He recognized that deducting a charge from operating profits for the cost of capital would force line managers to think more critically about the equipment they were adding. Like operating managers in many companies, they behaved as though equipment was free once they got the head office to approve the purchase. Brenn knew that attitude would quickly change if managers saw that their profit-and-loss statements included a sort of rental charge for the capital tied up in their operations, so he drafted a 10-page proposal touting the virtues of EVA and an EVA-linked bonus plan. "But we had a pretty good year in 1986, so my proposal went nowhere," he recalls. "I just filed it away in my desk."

Two years later, as capital outlays continued to swell and profits ebbed, CFO Eldridge took a closer look at EVA and its emphasis on capital accountability. He liked what he saw, and he and Brenn set out to convince Stratton of the merits of EVA. Stratton quickly agreed that EVA was the way to go. With his endorsement, the board voted unanimously to adopt EVA as its performance metric and as the basis for its incentive compensation. "We believe that this measurement, and incentive compensation linked to it, can effectively encourage management decisions that maximize the market value of capital contributed by investors," Stratton told shareholders at the 1991 annual meeting.

The new cash bonus plan, which initially covered 100 executives but now applies to every Briggs & Stratton employee, is based on achieving targeted dollar amounts of EVA improvement. If the company or a division achieves its targeted improvement, executives get their target bonuses, which range from 20% to 80% of base pay. Stratton also elected to include a feature of Stern Stewart EVA bonus plans that is used by most EVA companies today, but was rare in 1990: The management bonuses are uncapped, so that managers get a continuous percentage of whatever EVA improvement they achieve. The incentive plan had a powerful effect on Briggs executives, most of whom hadn't been eligible for any bonuses before then. "I understood the incentive plan long before I really understood EVA," says Paul Neylon, the general manager of Briggs's Spectrum (automotive components) division. "But at the foundry, we didn't call the incentives an EVA plan. We called it the Beemer plan." (Neylon got his BMW, though with two children in college he settled for a 325i.)

In 1993, Briggs & Stratton took its EVA incentives a step further by adding a leveraged stock option, or LSO, program for senior management. LSOs are options that managers must buy with a portion of their cash bonuses. They get options on far more shares than executives receive in conventional option plans, but these options have a couple of special twists. First, the number of options a manager gets is determined by the size of the EVA bonus. Second, the options have a rising exercise price, so managers don't profit from them unless shareholders get a good return on their investments. In other words, they don't pay off unless management performs. And if the stock performance is outstanding, managers reap enormous rewards. (See Chapter 7 for more on LSOs.)

With John Shiely intoning his mantra of "build, operate, and harvest," major changes began as soon as Briggs & Stratton went on EVA. The mantra refers to the three ways that operating executives can improve EVA: "build" by making new investments that promise to return more than the cost of capital, "operate" more efficiently to increase cash earnings without increasing the capital employed in the business, and "harvest" operations that aren't earning their cost of capital and do not have a decent prospect of doing so. The reorganization that Stratton put in place, coupled with divisional measurement of EVA—and divisional accountability for EVA—quickly brought big savings from harvesting. "We had some operations that were value killers for us," says Shiely. "We unloaded a captive starter motor business and a captive plastics molding operation after concluding that neither of them could earn the cost of capital in the hands of a *FORTUNE* 500 company." As noted above, Briggs also stopped making its premium Vanguard engines, buying them at lower cost from another manufacturer while simultaneously freeing $70 million of capital to be used more productively in other operations.

The double-barreled result was a simultaneous increase in operating profits and a reduction in capital and, in turn, capital costs. In its first four years on EVA, Briggs achieved a 28% increase in revenues with virtually no increase in net operating capital. Accounting profits moved back into the black in 1990, and by 1992 EVA also was positive to the tune of $2 million, up $64 million in just three years. Briggs & Stratton's return on capital rose from minus 1.2% in 1989 to plus 11.2% in 1992. Return on capital hit 20.2%—and EVA reached $38 million—in 1994. (See Figure 2.1.)

Shiely, who was the company's general manager at the time of the EVA implementation, immediately turned his attention to ways of taking the emphasis on EVA deep into the organization. If Fred

Figure 2.1

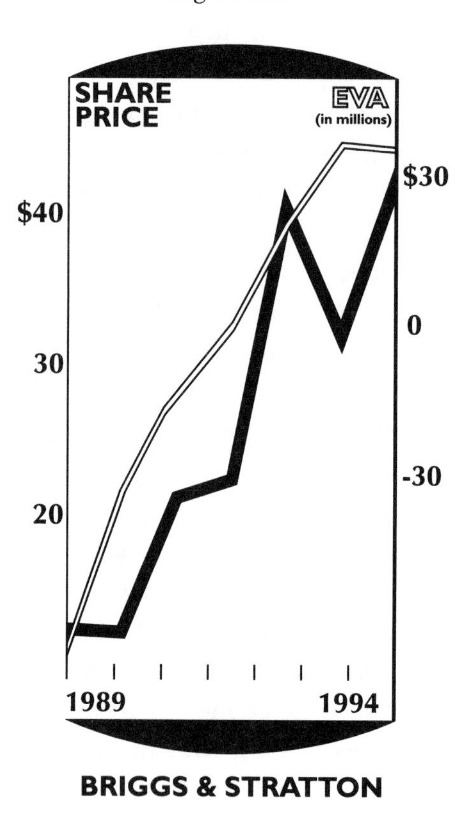

BRIGGS & STRATTON

Stratton was eager to make his managers think like owners, Shiely was equally intent on making workers think like managers. Shiely knew that continuing improvement in EVA would require continuing improvements in operations at all levels. As the company reengineered, he wanted everyone to understand that the real goal wasn't higher operating margins or lower defect rates or faster inventory turns or any of the other individual measures of operating efficiency. All those things matter, of course, but Shiely recognized that they matter only to the extent that they contribute to the greater goal of creating value by generating more EVA.

John Shiely has an uncommon grasp of the difference between accounting and the economics of business. Like Fred Stratton, he also has a familial attachment to Briggs & Stratton. His father spent a good part of his career there, and was chief executive for several years in the seventies. Shiely and Jim Wier, executive vice president of operations, quickly recognized that EVA gave them an opportunity to leverage their reengineering initiatives by educating shop-floor workers in the importance of capital costs. "EVA would give workers the cost accountability they needed to put this new manufacturing system to good use," says Shiely. "It's a reality you can track. We could have gone to cell manufacturing without EVA, but we would have fallen right back to where we were."

Wier wanted to put a halt to what he calls "managing by pushing on a balloon." By that, he refers to short-term initiatives that improve one driver of performance, but always at the expense of something else. One month the goal may be better management of raw materials inventories, but that leads to stock-outs and longer delivery times on orders, so the next month is total-customer-satisfaction month. Then the focus shifts to manufacturing efficiency, which can lead to higher inventories in order to facilitate longer production runs and lower unit production costs. Then it's right back to inventory management month, and so on. "I want our people to keep their focus on how all those drivers interact and affect each other and the bottom line," says Wier. "They do that by analyzing the EVA impact of every action they take."

Briggs & Stratton gives workers the tools to do that analysis by putting them through regular EVA training sessions. Judy Whipple, who runs the EVA instruction, teaches basic business economics by using domestic examples, such as equating the decision to replace an old, high-maintenance machine with the decision to replace a car that's aging. Will the savings in maintenance be big enough to offset the capital costs of a new car or machine? She also has her students play a game in which they operate a convenience store; the one with the highest EVA wins.

One example of how Shiely and Wier's shop-floor initiative has paid off comes from a casting facility in Ravenna, Michigan, that opened in 1995. The factory produces castings for camshafts and crankshafts used in Briggs & Stratton engines and supplies castings to other makers of automobiles, agricultural equipment, pumps, and compressors. Shiely approved the $23-million investment in Ravenna partly to meet the growing demand from outside buyers. Ed Bednar, general manager of the plant, has overall responsibility for its EVA. Since he is the one who best understands what drives EVA at the plant, he was also given the authority to mold its EVA incentive system as he saw fit. Bednar recalls with a smile how several new hires asked, "If this is a new factory, how come we have this used forklift running around the floor? And why all the used furniture?" Bednar told them that they would understand once they had gone through the mandatory EVA training.

In structuring the shop-floor incentives, Bednar drew on his long experience in casting to define the drivers of performance. He estimated that about 30% of the variability in the plant's EVA performance (at any given level of production) could be pegged directly to three variables under the control of individual work teams: molding efficiency, scrap rework, and attendance. First, as the term "molding efficiency" might suggest, mixing molten metal and molding it accurately is a delicate job. Workers able to do it efficiently avoid remolding, a time-consuming process that can scotch a delivery schedule. Next, when a casting emerges from the foundry, scrap—residue from the molding process—must be shaved off. Even a good molding job will have a minimal amount of scrap that must be removed by files and lathes. Only highly skilled teams can move production without turning out castings that need significant reworking. Third, the effect of good attendance on overall EVA is obvious. Making it a determinant of EVA bonuses gives a team member an extra incentive—and extra peer pressure—to show up for work.

"These are solid drivers," says Bednar. "If we have high molding efficiency—which means good utilization of assets—minimal scrap rework, and high attendance, good operational results will follow." Bednar concluded that those three drivers should determine 30% of the shop-floor bonuses, with the other 70% dependent on the plant's EVA. "We felt it wouldn't be fair to them to have the workers' bonus based 100% on plant EVA," he says. "Sales dollars could go up or down drastically for reasons outside workers' control. And good performance on the shop floor's 30% could help offset a slightly down year on the 70% side."

Bednar also decided that the EVA program for shop-floor incentives should be capped at 12% of annual salary. The uncapped bonuses that apply to most managers require the use of a bonus bank, with portions of exceptional bonuses withheld and subject to loss if EVA subsequently falls. The bonus bank is necessary to prevent managers from gaming the system by sacrificing long-term performance for short-term profitability. But Bednar reasoned that shop-floor workers would see a bonus bank as a management ruse to hold back bonuses they earned.

In educating the workers about EVA, trainers cited the used forklift as an example of wise capital management. If you can save $100,000 by buying used equipment, and your capital cost is 10%, that adds $10,000 a year to your EVA. The workers caught on quickly, even though most had never encountered any kind of incentive other than a profit-sharing plan. What took them by surprise was that the EVA plan could (and did) provide for a bonus payment in the first year, despite the fact that start-up costs kept the factory in the red. Since bonuses are based on achieving an expected level of EVA, an EVA that was less negative than anticipated would qualify for a bigger bonus. "Once they grasped that we would pay out a bonus even if there was negative EVA—that it was the growth in EVA that mattered—just about everyone became a believer," Bednar recalls.

It wasn't long before a proprietary interest in plant EVA began developing among the teams. While the plant manager, human resources manager, and accounting manager handle most of the calculation of EVA driver results that are posted around the plant each month, employees began monitoring some of the factors through their team activities. During quarterly meetings, Bednar and EVA facilitators—Briggs's term for designated team leaders responsible for seeing that EVA ideas reach management—would cover the material in detail. As these meetings progressed, Bednar says, it became clear that worker involvement had grown. He could see this in greater participation by individuals offering ideas. He also noted that a tangible feeling of competition filled the room. "All the team results are posted, so you know just who is responsible for a rise or fall in plant EVA."

The shop-floor discussions of EVA soon became quite sophisticated. One day in early 1996, two machine maintenance workers commented to a foreman that a conveyor belt transporting castings from the foundry to the cleaning facility suffered from constant jamming. They traced the problem to a magnetic separation device that lifted castings off one belt and onto another that delivered them to the cleaning room. The separator couldn't hoist the castings fast enough, causing the repeated fouling. The maintenance men, Eric Bamman and Kenneth Carrier, offered up a simple solution: Why not bypass the magnetic separator by extending one of the conveyors?

"The idea was not only that we could do away with jamming," says Bamman, "but also that we could reduce our capital by selling the separator and getting its value off our books." Carrier noted that the cost of the conveyor extension was minimal and could be done by the maintenance staff. Bednar gave them the go-ahead. The result? Downtime due to jams was reduced to less than one-half percent of work time and the capital charge for the machine is now off Ravenna's books. The sale also added to Briggs's cash flow. Says Shiely: "It's not only that these workers are thinking about capital costs for the first time. They have taken ownership of the plant and are acting on their ideas. That's EVA."

The new capital consciousness has produced similar improvements throughout Briggs & Stratton. Managers at the Burleigh Street factory used to buy perishable tools (ones that wear out in a short time) in large quantities in order to get the lowest unit price, and stored them in a huge crib. Briggs, of course, bore the cost of carrying the inventory of tools. Now managers at Burleigh Street buy from a single tool supplier, which was so pleased at getting the higher volume that it agreed to set up smaller cribs for each of the focus factories within Burleigh and shoulder the inventory costs itself. "They're happy because we've given them this huge volume of business," says operations manager Gary Zingler. "And we're happy because we don't have to carry the costs of the inventory." Zingler says the new arrangement has cut the costs for perishable-tools inventory by 82%. The change was an obvious one, of course, but it didn't happen until EVA—and EVA bonuses—focused operating managers on the capital they were using.

Taking EVA to the shop floor hasn't been all roses. In 1993 it precipitated a dispute with the company's union that took four years to resolve. In August of that year, as a $20-million redesign of the Burleigh factory neared completion, assemblers staged a work slowdown. At the time, Local 7232 of the United Paper Workers International was led by a group of militants who charged that the redesign and the new capital consciousness at Briggs would mean lost jobs and lost seniority. The work slowdown was part of an all-out "corporate campaign" against the company in which the union went so far as staging protests at Banc One, where Fred Stratton was a member of the board of directors, and charged that Briggs & Stratton's heartless policies were breaking up the marriages of workers, driving many to alcoholism and other substance abuse, and even threatened the life of the four-year-old daughter of a worker who was likely to lose his job and the insurance coverage that paid for life-sustaining drugs for the child.

By year-end 1993 the work slowdown had cost Briggs & Stratton $17 million and brought Shiely's shop-floor initiative to a halt. The union turned down an EVA-based bonus plan that would have netted its members considerable payouts. "We thought, what better way to drive a company than through value creation?" says Gerald Zitzer, vice president of human resources. "But for it to work well, you have to create value at every level, including the factory floor. It was tough to take EVA to the factory floor with the union dragging its feet."

Shiely opted to move more operations out of Wisconsin, and announced plans to build four new plants (including the Ravenna facility). He and Fred Stratton got pilloried in the local papers, and the leftist *National Catholic Reporter*, siding with the radical leadership of the union local, ran a story suggesting that they be excommunicated. "EVA is not always easy," admits Shiely. "It's tough to build new factories and then be vilified in the press for it." The *National Catholic Reporter* screed, accusing Briggs & Stratton's management of living in "denial and moral blindness," particularly upset Shiely, a Catholic who attended Marquette and Notre Dame. In response, the former altar boy composed a six-page philosophical treatise that rebutted the article and detailed the ethical grounding for EVA-based decisions. At one point in the letter, Shiely wrote, "We do not believe that any ethical or moral construct requires that Briggs & Stratton resign itself to the scrap heap of failed American corporations." When the paper refused to print his response, Shiely filed a $31-million libel suit. "It's like death by a thousand cuts," says Shiely. "You have to answer each and every cut."

The company's numbers showed that the new plants, despite investments totaling $120 million, would be EVA-positive within a few years. The same could not necessarily be said of the Burleigh plant, with its huge capital overhead and high labor costs, but Briggs & Stratton was determined to make the place work. In 1996 Briggs moved its Spectrum automotive components division from Menomonee Falls to Burleigh Street and sold the Menomonee Falls plant to Harley-Davidson. At first decried in the local press, the move eventually became recognized for the new beginning it was. Management had every intention of keeping the Burleigh plant, but transforming it into a workable, EVA-positive operation. As engine production moved to the new plants, Burleigh would add product lines that were less labor-intensive. Automotive components, for one, require little assembly.

"We think we can make Burleigh competitive in die casting and the components world," says controller Brenn. Adds operations manager Zingler: "We're getting the message out to our workers about the potential of the automotive components business. It could be huge for us." The workers got the message. So did the United Paper Workers International, which put Local 7232 in receivership and ousted the radical leaders. The members elected new leaders, who negotiated a bargaining agreement that the membership voted to accept in February 1997, effectively putting an end to the labor strife in Wauwautosa for five years. "With the changes we've made at the company, and now with the labor agreement, we have a real opportunity here at Burleigh," says a delighted Shiely. "And I'm not just talking about maintaining the business. We now have the chance to grow the business long-term."

Briggs & Stratton has even exported EVA to mainland China, where it has been manufacturing large cast-iron engines in a joint venture called Puyi Briggs & Stratton since the late 1980s. Puyi Briggs is located in Chongqing, a major iron and steel center that is the largest city in Sichuan province. The company was intrigued with getting a foothold in the People's Republic, although not for the lawn mower business. "They don't have much grass in China," explains Michael Hamilton, executive vice president of sales and service at Briggs. But China is close to Thailand and the Philippines, which made it a natural location for making the cast-iron engines. The engines are obsolete in industrial markets, but they provide excellent, cheap power for motorized outrigger canoes and rice paddy tillers.

Soon after implementing EVA at home, Briggs put 15 of its Chinese managers on an EVA bonus plan. "Those managers have done very well," says Hamilton. "Their performance factor is six" (meaning their bonuses are six times the target level). That, of course, makes the Chinese managers quite happy. "Chongqing is a very stable place," says Hamilton. "Very stable. And it has low wages. Actually, it's a lot like Pittsburgh."

After almost a decade of experience with EVA, John Shiely is one of its strongest proponents. "EVA is a very simple but elegant concept," he says. "A performance metric has to be two things—it has to be understandable and it has to be well linked to value. With a modicum of training, EVA can be understood by everyone, including people on the shop floor, and it motivates behavior that translates into a higher stock price for the company."

3

The Right Way to Keep Score

The most formidable obstacle many corporations face in their striving to create shareholder wealth is a fundamental misunderstanding of how the market sets stock prices. Ask any foursome of CEOs on the first tee at Pebble Beach what it takes to win in the wealth creation game, and at least three will say that the companies leading the field are those with either the highest total returns to shareholders or the highest market values. They also will tell you that the way to achieve a winning total return or market value is to produce rapid growth in earnings per share, preferably with the growth coming in a steady upward progression. And they'll be wrong on all counts. The facts are that total return to shareholders can be a misleading measure of performance, market value alone is meaningless, and *earnings per share don't count.*

Confusion over what drives stock prices is perfectly understandable for anyone who relies on daily press or television reports—or even on brokerage-house reports—for information about the market. As with so many things, much of the conventional wisdom about the stock market is dead wrong. Most of the "truths" you hear about the market—that quarterly earnings growth is what matters most; that investors, especially institutions, care only about short-term results; or that investor psychology drives the market—have little or nothing to do with reality. Even the language (especially the language) of market commentary is wildly off the mark. The next time you hear a panelist on *Wall Street Week* talking about the market consolidating gains, being overbought or oversold, or being overdue for a correction, change the channel. In these pages and in Chapter 5 we will give you a brief primer on how stocks really are valued, based on the findings of a legion of academic researchers who have produced a trove of empirical research on what determines market values. Those findings add up to a compelling case that a slavish devotion to earnings per share is a formula for wealth destruction, while managing for sustained increases in EVA is the best way to create shareholder wealth.

So what does constitute winning in the wealth creation game? Total return to shareholders certainly seems like the logical answer. After all, for any given company, a higher total return (price appreciation plus dividends) obviously is better than a lower one. But total return doesn't really tell you whether one company is doing better than another. That's because a company's required rate of return, or cost of capital, rises with the riskiness of the underlying business. Investors, for example, rightfully expect much higher returns from Genentech than from Con Edison, not because Genentech is a better stock (though it may be), but because biotech is a lot riskier than the regulated utility industry.

What's more, the required rate of return to equity investors rises with the degree of leverage in a company's balance sheet. Two companies in the same industry will have very different required rates of return to shareholders if one has no debt and the other has borrowed to the hilt. Because of these differences in risk levels, it is entirely possible that a company with a total return to shareholders of, say, 13% has performed better than another company with a total return of 15% or even 20%. To determine which company really is the superior performer, you have to go through a complicated process of "risk-adjusting" total returns according to each company's business risk and degree of financial leverage.

Even then, you cannot always be certain which is the better performer. Total return calculations assume that shareholders reinvest dividends, but the shareholders in any one company cannot all reinvest their dividends. One group of shareholders can reinvest dividends only to the extent that another group sells shares. Consider two companies with the same market capitalization, the same risk, and the same total return. Further, assume that any dividends shareholders receive are reinvested outside the company at a rate of return equal to the cost of capital. Shareholders are better off with the company that reinvests more of its earnings if the two companies' total returns are greater than their costs of capital, but they are better off with the one that pays out more in dividends if their returns are less than the cost of capital. In other words, if the two companies' total returns are greater than their costs of capital and one pays no dividends while the other pays a large dividend, the former company has created more wealth. If their total returns are less than the cost of capital, the latter has created more wealth (actually, it has destroyed less wealth).

Market value says nothing at all about wealth creation. It tells you the value of a company, of course, but it ignores the vital matter of how much capital the company invested to achieve that value. Wealth creation is determined not by the market value of a company, but by the *difference* between market value and the capital that investors have committed to the company. If each dollar of capital that a company invests (with money raised from equity offerings, retained earnings, or borrowings) produces less than a dollar of market value, that company is eroding the wealth of its shareholders. Shareholders would be better off with a dollar of dividends than with a dollar of retained earnings that adds only 80 cents to market value. And the bigger such a company grows, the more wealth it destroys. But a company that sells at a premium over its invested capital has created wealth. That company has passed what might be called the "Buffett test," as explained by legendary investor Warren Buffett in the 1984 annual report of his Berkshire Hathaway Corporation: "We believe noble intentions should be checked periodically against results. We test the wisdom of retaining earnings by assessing whether retention, over time, delivers at least $1 of market value for each $1 retained."

For a vivid illustration of what we mean, take a look at Dell Computer Corporation and Digital Equipment Corporation. The two computer makers were running almost neck-and-neck in market value at the end of 1996, yet Dell is a stellar wealth creator while DEC was a signal wealth destroyer. Dell had achieved a market value of $8.7 billion with a capital base of just $418 million, which means it had created $8.3 billion of shareholder wealth (the $8.7 billion market value minus $418 million of capital). DEC, in contrast, had invested nearly $12 billion to produce only $8.1 billion of market value; it had destroyed $3.9 billion of shareholder wealth. Little wonder, then, that DEC has since been acquired by Compaq Computer Corporation.

The difference between total market value (of both equity and debt) and total capital is a figure we call MVA, for *market value added*. The formula is simple:

$$\text{MVA} = \text{market value} - \text{total capital}$$

MVA is the definitive measure of wealth creation. It beats out all other measures because it is the difference between cash in and cash out—between what investors put into a company as capital and what they could get out by selling at today's market price. As such, MVA is the cumulative amount by which a company has enhanced—or diminished—shareholder wealth. MVA also is the best external measure of management performance because it captures the market's assessment of the effectiveness with which a company's managers have used the scarce resources under their control. MVA also reflects how well management has positioned the company for the long term, because market values incorporate the present value of expected long-run payoffs.

What's more, MVA is automatically risk-adjusted, because the market values of companies incorporate investor judgments about risk as well as performance. This means that MVA is a measure you can use to directly compare the performance of companies in different industries or even different countries. You can use MVA to compare, say, a bank and a retailer or a steelmaker and a software company. The one with the higher MVA has created more wealth, period. Most important, MVA is the ultimate goal in the wealth creation game. The overarching financial objective of every company should be to create as much shareholder wealth—as much MVA—as possible. As Coke's Roberto Goizueta told *FORTUNE* magazine, "It's the way to keep score. Why everyone doesn't use it is a mystery to me."

MVA is exactly equivalent to the stock market's estimate of the net present value, or NPV, of a company. For those who aren't familiar with the term, NPV is the end result of what is known as the discounted cash flow method of valuing an investment. This is a method of analyzing prospective investment projects that most corporations use in their capital budgeting. It is a calculation that discounts all expected future cash flows from a project back to the present at an interest rate that reflects the time value of money and the riskiness of the project—in other words, at the cost of capital. Subtracting all the investment outlays necessary to produce those discounted cash flows yields the net present value of the project. One of the first principles of modern corporate finance is that companies should undertake all projects with positive NPVs—all projects where expected returns exceed the cost of capital—and reject any project whose NPV is negative.

If you think of a corporation as an agglomeration of investment projects, MVA is the stock market's estimate of the aggregate net present value of all those projects—both those already in place *and those that investors anticipate will be undertaken in the future.* In the same way that an NPV calculation subtracts the up-front investment required to fund a project from the present value of anticipated cash flows, the MVA calculation takes a company's gross market value and subtracts the cumulative capital investment made to date. What's left over is the net present value of the company. One way that managers can get a read on whether their own stock is over- or undervalued is to make their own estimate of the aggregate NPV of the company and compare it with the company's MVA. Then, of course, they have to ask why the market's judgment differs from their own: Do they have superior, inside information, or is the market being more objective?

MVA is a company's market value minus the book value of its invested capital, but you can't use accounting book value to calculate MVA accurately. That's because generally accepted accounting principles (GAAP) often deviate from economic reality, and almost always in ways that tend to understate the amount of capital a company has invested. GAAP requires companies to do a number of wrongheaded things, such as writing off all research and development expenditures in the year they are made and amortizing goodwill from acquisitions (goodwill is the difference between the purchase price of an acquired company and the "fair value" of its assets). In economic terms, all cash outlays that are expected to contribute to future earnings, such as R&D, should be added to capital instead of being expensed. So spending on R&D should be added to the balance sheet and written off over time because it represents an investment in future products or processes. Goodwill shouldn't be written off at all.

In calculating MVA, Stern Stewart makes these adjustments and others like them to convert accounting book value into an *economic* book value, or what it calls capital. As one example, Eli Lilly, an EVA company, had an accounting book value of $6 billion at the end of 1996, and an economic book value, or capital, of $13.1 billion.

Some $2.1 billion of the difference represented the capitalized value of R&D spending in prior years. Another $4 billion was previously amortized goodwill. In effect, capital is what book value would be if accountants were financial economists. We'll get back to the problems with earnings later on. Suffice it to say here that accounting earnings suffer from the same GAAP-related maladies as book value, which is one reason why earnings are such a poor gauge of performance and demonstrably are *not* what drive stock prices or MVA.

Stern Stewart has prepared an annual MVA ranking of the largest nonfinancial U.S. companies, called the Stern Stewart Performance 1000, for nearly a decade, and it has been ranking companies in other countries as well in recent years. *FORTUNE* has published the U.S. Performance 1000 since 1993, and other leading periodicals around the globe publish the MVA rankings for their countries, including the *Sunday Times* in the United Kingdom, *Capital* in Germany, *L'Expansion* in France, the *Financial Post* in Canada, *Exame* in Brazil, and *Reforma* and *El Norte* in Mexico. The statement in Chapter 1 that Coca-Cola became the No. 1 wealth creator in the world in 1994 referred to the fact that it became the No. 1 company on the Performance 1000 that year. By the end of 1996 Coke had achieved a market value of $135.7 billion with just $10.8 billion of capital, for an MVA of $124.9 billion. Others in the top ranks of the MVA list include such household names as Microsoft, Intel, Merck, and Procter & Gamble. Significantly, and unsurprisingly, the companies that lead the Performance 1000 also show up at the top of *FORTUNE*'s annual survey of corporate reputations.

Unlike other popular rankings of companies, which focus on sales, market value, or other measures of sheer size, the Performance 1000 and its siblings have real meaning as measures of corporate success because they rank companies by the dollar amount of shareholder wealth they have created or destroyed. The *FORTUNE* 500, which ranks companies by sales, includes a profusion of other data, including earnings, earnings growth, rate of return on equity, and total return to shareholders. All those numbers are interesting, but they tell you remarkably little about the crucial matter of wealth creation.

Consider the statistics on General Motors, which had revenues of $168 billion in 1996 and is perennially No. 1 on the *FORTUNE* 500. GM's 1996 earnings of $5 billion were the fifth highest on the *FORTUNE* list and $1.5 billion higher than Coke's. Its return on equity was No. 103. It even ranked in the top half—No. 238—in 10-year growth in earnings per share. A pretty respectable performance, right? Wrong. GM has consistently been at or near the bottom of the Performance 1000, and was dead last at the end of 1996. With $82.9 billion of invested capital and a market value of just $62.2 billion, GM had an MVA of *minus* $20.7 billion. It had destroyed more shareholder wealth than any other company.

Now take a look at Coke, which came in at No. 58 on the *FORTUNE* 500 with 1996 revenues of $18.5 billion. Its 10-year growth in earnings per share was only 57th on the 500—much better than GM but still a long way from No. 1. And Coke's total return to investors ranked 18th over 10 years and 89th in 1996. Many of the companies that bested Coke by this measure were in riskier businesses. More important, most didn't create anywhere near the amount of shareholder wealth over those 10 years. Oracle, No. 1 in 10-year total return, created $23.5 billion of MVA. United HealthCare, No. 12, created $5.6 billion of MVA. Coca-Cola's MVA shot up by $114.2 billion over the same period. In short, no conventional performance measure—or any combination of them—reveals the fact that Coca-Cola was the greatest wealth creator, and GM the greatest wealth destroyer, as of the end of 1996. Only MVA answers capitalism's most fundamental question: By what amount has management increased or diminished the value of the capital entrusted to it?

Like market value, MVA is a snapshot at a given point in time. It is the amount of wealth a company has created or destroyed since its inception. From the standpoint of assessing the performance of current management, the change in MVA over a period of one year or five years can be more significant than the absolute level of MVA. An increase in MVA means that the company's market value grew by more than any additional funds raised or retained from earnings. A decrease in MVA, on the other hand, spells trouble because it means that shareholder wealth has been eroded.

Changes in MVA can be caused by a variety of factors. All stocks, for example, tend to rise and fall with the overall market. Over the five years from the end of 1991 to the end of 1996, when the market rose beyond almost all expectations (and then kept on going up), the aggregate MVA of the companies on the Performance 1000 grew more than 150%, from $1.2 trillion to $3.1 trillion. (The aggregate MVA at the end of 1981, eight months before the beginning of the great bull market, was minus $70 billion.) But stocks don't all move together in lockstep. In 1996, a great year for stocks overall, about one quarter of the companies on the Performance 1000 suffered declines in MVA. Most companies also are buffeted by the winds affecting their particular industries. In 1996, for instance, most telecommunications and entertainment companies took big MVA hits, while most companies in the computer, software, drug, personal care, and oil and gas industries were big winners.

The most important factor driving MVA, however, is management. Ultimately, what determines a company's fate isn't the industry it happens to be in, but the rightness of its strategy and the excellence with which management executes that strategy. That fact is especially clear in the computer industry, where radical differences in MVA performance abound. Dell, for example, has marched steadily upward on the Performance 1000 in the nineties, rising from No. 528 at the end of 1991 to No. 67 at the end of 1996 as its MVA shot from $290 million to $8.3 billion. Compaq's ascent has been even more stunning, from No. 933 to No. 51 (from an MVA of minus $284 million to a positive $12.8 billion) in just five years. Over those same years, in contrast, Apple Computer, Inc., tumbled from No. 97 to No. 987 as its MVA went from $3.2 billion to minus $1.2 billion.

Such contrasts aren't limited to computer companies. Wal-Mart, even after four dreadful years following the death of founder Sam Walton, was No. 14 (MVA: $34.7 billion) on the Performance 1000 at the end of 1996, while Kmart was No. 996 (minus $2.2 billion), down from No. 153 five years before. In the tobacco industry, Philip Morris held the No. 6 position ($66.6 billion) and RJR Nabisco was No. 999 (minus $12 billion). Now look at beverages, generally one of the best businesses almost everywhere in the world. Companhia Cervejaria Brahma, the large Brazilian brewer and soft-drink bottler—and the first company in that country to adopt EVA—tops the Brazilian performance ranking at $3.2 billion of MVA. Even PepsiCo, which runs a very poor second to Coke in soft drinks, was No. 17 on the U.S. ranking with an MVA of $32 billion at the end of 1996. And Anheuser-Busch, the world's largest brewer, was No. 48. Yet it is possible to do badly in beverages. Adolph Coors Company proves it with an MVA rank of No. 969.

The contrast between General Motors and Chrysler Corporation also shows that industry isn't necessarily destiny, and that it is possible to do comparatively well even in a bad business. Faced with worldwide overcapacity in the auto industry in the eighties, GM responded by starting a whole new company—Saturn Corporation—to make even more cars, alienated employees by spending tens of billions of dollars on robots and other automation it could never get to work right, and mollified its unions by offering extremely generous postretirement benefit payments. In the decade from 1986 to 1996 GM remained at the bottom of the Performance 1000 as it destroyed an additional $2.5 billion of shareholder wealth.

Chrysler, meanwhile, adopted total quality management successfully early on, exited the auto business in Europe, led the move to minivans and sport-utility vehicles, sped up the time to develop new cars, and created exciting new concept cars like the Dodge Viper and Plymouth Pronto Spyder to inspire employees and customers. In the

10 years ended in 1996, Chrysler created $3.5 billion of shareholder wealth and rose from the cellar to No. 200 on the Performance 1000. And, in the most damning comparison for GM, Toyota is No. 1 in MVA in Japan.

In thinking about MVA, it is helpful to keep in mind that stock prices are purely expectational. That is, the value of a stock depends entirely on the profits that investors expect a company to produce in the future. Past profits matter only because they are an important factor driving expectations about future performance. Past capital investments—what economists call "sunk costs"—are irrelevant. The value of a project, or a company, is determined by the cash that investors expect to get out of it, not what has already gone into it. In the stock market, the real question isn't "What have you done for me lately?" It's "What are you going to do for me tomorrow?"

Here's how expectations affect MVA. A company's market value is the present value of future profits discounted to today at the company's cost of capital. If investors expect a company to earn exactly its cost of capital, and no more or no less, then its market value will be exactly equal to capital. In this case, MVA—market value minus capital—will be zero. Wealth is preserved when investors expect a company to generate enough profits to meet the minimum acceptable rate of return. If expected returns exceed the cost of capital, the company's stock will sell at a premium and MVA will be positive; management has created wealth by convincing investors that it will produce profits that exceed the cost of capital. If expected returns amount to less than the cost of capital, management has destroyed wealth and MVA will be negative.

This may be clearer if you think about profits in the context of interest payments on a bond. If market interest rates on government bonds currently are 6%, this is the cost of capital on government bonds. If a bond issued several years ago has an interest coupon of 7.5%, the bond will sell at more than its par value. That is, it will be priced in the market so that the interest payments and the final repayment of principal work out to a 6% return on the current market value. If the coupon is less than 6%, it will sell at a discount. All financial instruments are valued in the market on this basis. The relationship is more difficult to grasp when it comes to stocks because future profits, unlike interest payments on a bond, are not fixed. But the dynamics are the same.

While the goal of every company should be to create as much MVA as possible, MVA itself is not much use as a guide to day-to-day decision making. For one thing, changes in the overall level of the stock market can overwhelm the contribution of management actions in the short run. Second, MVA can be calculated only if a company is publicly traded and has a market price. Third, even for public companies, MVA can be calculated only at the consolidated level; there is no MVA for a division, business unit, subsidiary, or product line. Thus, MVA provides no help in assessing the performance of the many pieces that make up the corporate whole. As a result, managers have to focus on some *internal* measure of performance that is closely linked to the *external* MVA verdict.

The vast majority of companies use earnings per share as their primary internal measure of success. The widespread reliance on accounting earnings as the worldly grail has obvious causes, of course. The Securities and Exchange Commission requires all public companies to report earnings as computed according to GAAP. Securities analysts traditionally have spent much of their time trying (demonstrably unsuccessfully) to predict earnings, and couch their reports and valuations in terms of anticipated earnings and earnings per share. The financial press focuses on earnings as the ultimate benchmark of performance, and correspondents on CNBC and CNN/fn report daily on stocks that took a beating because the latest earnings reports came in below consensus expectations. So most companies make higher earnings their primary financial goal, and base their incentive compensation for top management on targets for growth in earnings or earnings per share.

As you will see, this blind faith in earnings (blind because there is absolutely no convincing evidence that earnings drive shareholder wealth, and an abundance of evidence to the contrary) is a huge mistake. It leads companies to continually shoot their shareholders in the foot by taking actions that boost reported profits but destroy value. The far better course is to manage for increases in EVA, because EVA is the internal performance measure that is most highly correlated with MVA and provides the most reliable guide to whether—and by how much—management actions will contribute to shareholder wealth.

4

How EVA Reshaped Armstrong World Industries and Boise Cascade

No self-respecting management team ever looks forward to a hostile takeover bid or a major onslaught by activist shareholders, but a few can look back with satisfaction on ones where they prevailed. Two members of this select group are Armstrong World Industries and Boise Cascade Corporation. Armstrong was the object of a tender offer in 1989 by the Belzbergs, the Canadian family notorious as skillful corporate raiders, while Boise had the unfortunate distinction of making it onto CalPERS's hit list of companies sorely in need of governance reform in February 1995. In the years since, both companies have performed well for shareholders and won accolades for the quality of their corporate governance. They also happen to have adopted EVA as a way to keep managers focused squarely on creating shareholder wealth.

By any reckoning, Armstrong has been on a roll. The company, which sells more than $2 billion a year of its floor coverings, insulation, and ceiling and wall systems, won a Baldrige award for quality in 1995. The following year, *Chief Executive* magazine named its board one of the five best in America, citing Armstrong's

28.5% average return to shareholders for three years running, an ambitious approach to corporate governance, and its use of EVA as the basis for incentive compensation. Ironically, some of the credit for Armstrong's recent successes and its conversion to EVA has to go to the Belzbergs. During the seventies and eighties, Armstrong's financial and stock performance had been on a roller-coaster ride. By 1989 the Belzbergs thought they spied the chance for a quick profit and went after the company with a tender offer to be financed with junk bonds. Like most target companies, Armstrong went all out to defend itself, but what finally thwarted the raiders was the collapse of the junk-bond market. With their financing suddenly cut off, the Belzbergs launched a proxy fight instead, putting up three candidates for Armstrong's board of directors.

Dissident candidates for a company board are notoriously hard to elect, but Armstrong, a great believer in corporate democracy, employed cumulative voting, which gives shareholders one vote per share for each board seat up for election and allows them to put all their votes behind one or two candidates. The system is designed to aid minority representation, and in this case one of the Belzberg candidates was elected. The winner was no Evelyn Davis, no nutty gadfly who loudly disputes the chairman and provides comic relief at annual shareholders meetings. The new director was Michael C. Jensen, the Harvard finance professor who has done seminal work on agency costs and the theory of the firm and is a radical proponent of managing for shareholder value.

Armstrong took a particularly heavy battering in the 1990–1991 recession. Part of the problem was that the company is in a cyclical industry that moves in tandem with the cycles in commercial and residential construction, and commercial construction was in a virtual depression in those years. But Armstrong's downswing was deepened by some weak business segments that steadily eroded the capital invested in them. At this point the board, and Jensen in particular, began to have a substantial impact on getting the company to think about finding a better way to measure performance and reward success. "Jensen's whole point was that a company had to earn more than its cost of capital, and he pounded the table and made us listen," recalls assistant treasurer Warren Posey.

Jensen's exhortations in the boardroom led to a white paper by Posey arguing that accounting goals are not the way to drive shareholder value. "We concluded that there was no reason to continue using return on assets as a concept," says Posey. "We had to use a value-driving performance measure." The company set up a five-man task force of finance executives to explore new techniques to enhance value. After months of study, the task force recommended EVA as the optimal performance metric. Jensen strongly advocated the change, as did George Lorch, who became CEO of Armstrong in September 1993. At its meeting that month, the board approved the change to EVA.

Since late 1994, management has been setting EVA targets for each of the company's 14 business units as well as for the corporation as a whole. In many cases, EVA targeting goes down to subdivisions within a business unit. Managers receive monthly EVA reports, tracking performance against the target for the month, the year to date, and the prior year. EVA quickly showed its utility, says CFO Frank Riddick, as "a balance sheet and operating measure all in one." And the new compensation system, tied to EVA results, was the spur to fresh creativity and innovation. The EVA incentive system covers all salaried staff in the United States and abroad. The top corporate officers receive a bonus based 100% on Armstrong's overall EVA performance. The heads of business units generally get 30% of their bonus determined by overall corporate performance and 70% from their unit's score. Managers below them are 100% dependent on their unit EVAs.

Lorch and his team in the executive suite faced a major challenge in clearing away debris left behind by prior regimes. The company has an illustrious history, but at times it went off on unprofitable tangents. Founded in 1860 as the Armstrong Cork Company, a manufacturer of cork stoppers for all sorts of bottles, the company got into the linoleum floor business early in this century (cork shavings mixed with linseed oil produce linoleum) and later branched out into ceilings, pipe insulation, and other odds and ends. In the 1960s, management adopted the slogan "Creators of the indoor world," the logic of which, in the era of conglomeration, led to the purchase of a carpet business, a furniture company, and a ceramic tile operation known as American Olean. All this acquisitiveness bespoke synergy and great corporate vision, but it consistently damaged the company's overall economic performance. The carpet business was shed in 1989, even before EVA; it clearly was an underperformer by any measure.

The cleanup campaign began in earnest with the adoption of EVA. Examining the EVA position of the entire company, Riddick remembers asking, "Where the hell is all the EVA going? Where's the leakage?" Analysis showed that floor coverings, ceilings, and insulation products added substantially to value, while American Olean and Thomasville Furniture Industries were huge drains. Olean had been bought at too high a price and had been consistently unprofitable.

One option was to close it down, another to expand by buying a competitor, a third to sell it. The company's analysis indicated that acquisition and expansion could have been a successful strategy, but Lorch rejected it. "We had $400 million in capital tied up and had never made a nickel out of it," he says. "For me, first thing out of the box, to put $800 or $900 million into a business we had never made any money in? They would have given me a saliva test." Instead, he sold Olean in 1995 to Dal-Tile, a leading competitor, in exchange for 37% of the latter's shares. The result has been a dependable income stream and has been regarded as a great success.

By contrast, Thomasville Furniture had been consistently profitable on an accounting basis since its purchase, but it had never earned its cost of capital. In its final year, it had an operating profit of only $40 million on sales of $500 million, and ended up with a negative EVA of $5 million. The problem, according to Riddick, was that Thomasville was in the high end of the furniture business, where each product is virtually made to order, which forecloses significant production efficiencies and requires substantial investments in inventory. Margins were just too low to provide adequate profits. One possible solution was to expand into the retail end of the business. But that gambit seemed risky because the bankruptcy rate is high among furniture retailers and the business would have been an unfamiliar one to Armstrong. Another strategy was to grow by buying up other furniture manufacturers. "We rejected that," says Riddick, "because no one has been successful doing that so far." In the end, Armstrong sold Thomasville to Interco for $338 million. For Thomasville to have earned its cost of capital on the sale price, it would have had to consistently produce operating income of $60 million or more, something Riddick saw as an impossible goal. "Clearly, it was worth more to someone else than to us," says Riddick.

EVA analysis has also been crucial in evaluating potential acquisitions (so far no major ones have passed the test) as well as the feasibility of Armstrong's internal expansion plans. EVA led Riddick to nix a plan to put a vinyl flooring plant in China. Though a corporate presence in China is all the rage these days (Armstrong already had one as a manufacturer of ceiling tile in Shanghai), Riddick was adamant. "We rejected it because it would have negative EVA. It would cost us $80 million and the market isn't developed enough to have the plant pay off, so we have to put these plans on hold. We're getting into that market by importing."

Of greater significance is Armstrong's "consensus" decision not to build new factories in North America. "We're saying," says Riddick, "that we're probably better off putting in productivity improvements in existing plants. EVA forced the operating guys to say, 'It would be easier to build a new plant, but you know what might happen if we go into a downturn two years from now. We'd be stuck with a lot of excess capacity we can't use, and while our profits won't be hurt that much, in terms of EVA we'll be killed.'"

A new factory to manufacture mineral board ceilings was the specific issue in 1996. The new facility looked attractive until Armstrong concluded that it could achieve the same additional capacity at a quarter of the $60 to $80 million that a new plant would cost. Technological advances made that alternative possible. The old plant had four production lines—one to form the mineral board (made from a slurry of old newspapers and water), another to cut the board, a third to decorate it, and a fourth to package it—all operating at different speeds. The different production rates gave rise to considerable work-in-process inventory and a lot of shuffling of materials from one line to a holding area and then on to another line. Now, through the use of new techniques that use bigger motors and require less water, each process can move along at the same speed. The result is a continuous production line, greatly increased output on each shift, and lower inventory and handling costs.

Managers of business units speak with enthusiasm of what EVA has meant in their areas. Robert Shannon, Jr., president of worldwide floor products operations—responsible for 50% of the entire corporate volume—explains how EVA shaped Armstrong's debut into the Central European and Russian markets. In the past, the company would have built factories or entered joint ventures in which it insisted on being the dominant partner. "In the old Armstrong," Shannon recalls, "they wouldn't do deals if they didn't own 50%. Now we seek to define the minimum amount of capital that we can put into a deal and still get what we want out of it. As a result, we've been able to build a business in Europe that now has a very strong EVA, earning roughly twice its cost of capital." In some cases Armstrong has taken a minority position in joint ventures or bought 30% of the shares in an existing company. It now has operations in Poland, Serbia, and Russia and a controlling interest in Holmsund Golv AB, a Swedish flooring manufacturer.

Shannon says EVA also persuaded some of his managers to relinquish prerogatives they zealously, and expensively, defended in the past. One of Armstrong's British plants and the one in Serbia produce floor tiles with the same designs. It takes three or more embossing cylinders to apply each design one color at a time. Each cylinder costs around three thousand dollars, and Armstrong uses dozens of designs. When not in use, the cylinders sit in storage. The normal procedure would be for each plant to have a full complement of cylinders so that it could fill any order. But the British manager thought this was ridiculous. Put them on a truck and ship them back and forth, he said. They did it, and reaped savings to the tune of six figures.

EVA infuses every aspect of operations at corporate retail accounts, which sells and services the so-called big box chain retailers like Home Depot. Stephen E. Stockwell, president of the division, has sold his 140-member workforce on the proposition that lots of small savings add up to big ones, with a palpable impact on the monthly EVA scorecard and their annual compensation. Nowhere is this more apparent than in the division's record on receivables. All companies try to keep the life of receivables as short as possible, of course, but corporate retail accounts has been doing a significantly better job since it went on EVA.

The matter first comes up when a salesperson negotiates a deal with a customer, involving price, credit terms, cooperative advertising, and incentives if sales go over a certain volume. Prior to EVA, salespeople were likely to be generous with payment terms in order to clinch the sale. They were compensated, after all, on their sales volume. No longer. The division's EVA record determines their bonuses now. In the new era, the salesperson approaches the customer with an arithmetic model in hand for each element in the sale and plugs in the numbers to see what can be afforded without the deal plunging into negative EVA. The impact of this discipline has been dramatic. At the end of 1994, the average age of receivables in corporate retail accounts was 42.7 days. By the end of 1996, it was down to 38.4 days—a reduction of 10%. This translates into a hefty chunk of dollars in a business doing an annual volume of over $400 million.

Armstrong's new focus on earning more than its cost of capital has paid off. Anyone who invested $100 at the end of 1992 and reinvested dividends would have had an investment worth $269 by December 31, 1997, better performance than that of the S&P 500 and considerably better than Armstrong's peer group. Says Michael Jensen, who left the Armstrong board once the EVA implementation was complete: "Armstrong is a company with great products, people, and culture. But its organizational rules of the game were poor, and the result was lots of value destruction. Introducing EVA changed both the performance measurement and the compensation systems, which then drove significant changes in business practices that generated huge increases in value."

While Armstrong has prospered, Boise Cascade has been whipsawed throughout the nineties, a victim of the incredible price swings—mostly downward—that have plagued the paper business. When the company first came into CalPERS's sights in 1994, it had fared worse than many of its competitors during a prolonged slump. "If you looked at its peers, you could see that Boise had a lot of things to improve," says one financial analyst. That's precisely what it has been doing since adopting EVA at the beginning of 1995. Boise's stock shot up 31% in 1995 as a recovery in paper prices and the implementation of EVA brought a dramatic upswing in performance. Another collapse in paper prices sent profits plunging again in 1996, but not, says CEO George Harad, by as much as they would have fallen prior to Boise's implementation of EVA. Boise even managed to boost EVA by $60 million in 1997, yet another dreadful year for its industry. The improvements are the product of Boise's strategy to earn its cost of capital over the business cycle by moving out of the EVA-challenged commodity paper business and expanding in areas such as value-added paper and office products.

Boise's senior management had begun asking tough questions of itself well before the company made the CalPERS dishonor roll. There were plenty of reasons for doing so. The paper industry went into one of its regular slumps in the early nineties, but this one didn't stop. Paper prices dropped through the floor and stayed there. By 1994, Boise's pretax EVA was minus $563 million (the company is one of the few that calculates EVA on a pretax basis). The year before, Boise had established a committee to investigate alternative performance measures as a way to get better control of costs, and the group soon settled on EVA. "We figured that with EVA we could get our managers to start thinking about their balance sheets and not just their P&Ls," says controller Thomas Carlile, who cochaired the committee. The balance sheet weighs far more heavily in forest products than it does in most industries. Boise, for example, owns or controls more than three million acres of timberland, and a single machine for making uncoated sheet paper can cost upwards of $400 million. "A capital-intensive business?" muses J. Michael Gwartney, vice president for human resources. "It's like going to war."

Gwartney says EVA's simplicity was a major selling point: "There's no use having a measurement if people don't know how it works. Other measures are like bowling pins with a blanket over them. You roll the ball, you hear the noise, but you don't know what's happening. The real kick about EVA is that employees can do something with it." Harad, who became CEO in 1994, made his own study of EVA and accepted the measurement committee's recommendation.

The greatest change at Boise has been that shift in its business mix away from commodity papers and into value-added papers and office products. It has spun off its newsprint and coated publication-paper businesses and closed an inefficient pulp-and-paper facility in Vancouver, Washington. Boise also has been rebuilding a plant in Jackson, Alabama, to convert it from a paper-and-pulp operation to paper only, eliminating the unattractive, low-margin pulp production. In addition, Boise has been expanding rapidly in the distribution business, particularly in office products, where Harad sees much greater opportunity to generate positive EVA.

Since 1993 office products sales have grown from 16% of total revenues to 44%, while paper's share of revenues has dropped from 46% to 27%.

Among other things, EVA has affected the way Boise buys timber. The company obtains most of its raw material under arrangements called timber under contract, or TUCs. Under a TUC, the company makes an up-front payment for the right to cut timber from private land over a preset period that typically runs from one to three years. The practice protects the company from swings in the price of gatewood, the lumberman's term for logs bought from a contractor, but it also ties up substantial capital. When Boise went on EVA, managers had to factor a 16% capital charge into all their analyses (since Boise measures EVA on a pretax basis, it uses a pretax cost of capital). The capital charge suddenly made the price protection built into TUCs look decidedly more expensive. As a result, managers began negotiating harder with landowners and entered into far fewer TUCs. "Our lumber inventory went down 30% in the first year and a half," says Thomas Lovelien, manager of one of Boise's five timber regions. "That's a direct result of focusing on EVA."

EVA analysis also helped James Huff decide on the product mix at a pulp-and-paper mill in St. Helens, Oregon, after it was retooled to make value-added papers. The retooling followed five years of mill-level operating losses on commodity papers in the late eighties and early nineties. "EVA has been a good measuring tool in helping us decide which products we should have in our mix," says Huff. "We now are the second-highest EVA pulp-and-paper mill in the company." EVA also changed the operating strategy at St. Helens. "Our number one expense is the cost of wood chips," says Huff. In the past, incentive compensation at the mill was based on output. "If your incentive is output, you are going to have extra inventory," he says. "But once you're told you're paying for inventory—and at 16% no less—you'd better believe you keep inventory down." Instead of stockpiling chips, Huff now insists that vendors carry some of the inventory.

Some operating managers were skeptical about the move to EVA, which is not unusual in highly cyclical industries. For one thing, the operating managers had learned how to succeed under the old system, which used pretax rate of return on capital as the internal performance measure. A new system naturally was seen as a threat. What's more, Boise began its EVA incentive system in 1995, the first good year in five in the paper business. "All of a sudden, we changed the incentive plan just when things started to get better," says Gwartney. "When you do that, people's cynicism index starts to go up." To bring the index down, Boise let its operating managers take whichever bonus proved higher in 1995—the EVA bonus or whatever their bonus would have been under the old system. Corporate officers did not have a choice; they went on EVA. "What a tool to sell EVA to our people," says Gwartney. "Suddenly there's ownership by the officers."

As it turned out, the EVA bonus paid more—by far—than the old incentive compensation plan as Boise's EVA shot from minus $563 million in 1994 to plus $105 million in 1995. The huge increase in EVA produced bonuses that were 5.3 times target bonuses, but nearly half that award stayed in Boise's bonus bank, which it calls a smoothing pool.

Unfortunately, prices dropped right back down in 1996, and EVA tumbled to minus $478 million. Bad as that was, Boise management believes the company would have done much worse had it not made the change to EVA and begun changing its product mix. Then came the $60-million improvement in EVA in 1997 in the face of paper prices that continued downward in the first half and averaged only 3% higher than they had been in the trough year of 1993. Boise's expected improvement in the bonus plan is $40 million following a year in which EVA is negative and 0 when EVA is positive. Boise's smoothing pool—and the potential for negative bonuses—functioned precisely as they were supposed to in the boom and bust. After the bonuses of 5.3 times targets in 1995, the 1996 bonuses came in at *minus* 2.3 times target. In other words, the collapse in paper prices and EVA brought a deduction from the managers' smoothing-pool balances.

But even though bonuses were negative in 1996, managers got a modest payout equal to 50% of their remaining bonus-pool balances. It wasn't much—only 7.4% of the target bonus—but at least it was something; managers would have received zero under the old plan. Then, with the heroic EVA performance in 1997, managers got payouts of 1.16 times target bonuses, reflecting a combination of bonuses earned that year and a modest increment from the smoothing-pool balances.

5

Earnings per Share Don't Count—EVA Does

The first thing any company should do in its pursuit of a higher MVA is to abandon the cult of earnings per share. For one thing, companies are putting themselves through needless accounting gymnastics out of the mistaken belief that investors are myopic fools who care only about the latest quarterly earnings release. The presumption that companies can manipulate their stock prices by manufacturing earnings numbers is hubris at best, and leads to dishonesty at worst. What's more, the practice of constantly trying to please Wall Street with the "right" earnings number causes corporations to do all manner of dumb things.

Some of those things are simply silly, like ConAgra's boast in its 1997 annual report that its "17 consecutive years of earnings per share growth at a compound rate better than 14% is unequaled by any major food company in the United States, and probably in the world." That certainly would be worth trumpeting if it were true. But ConAgra had to fiddle the numbers to create the illusion of steadily increasing earnings. The fine print below a chart of its annual earnings increases reveals that the record conveniently excludes an accounting change for postretirement health benefits in 1993 and nonrecurring charges in 1983, 1984, and 1996. Instead of accolades, ConAgra's "record" got it a slap in the face. In a *FORTUNE* article that casts proper aspersions on the candor and integrity of ConAgra management, Carol Loomis noted that a box of grilled glazed pork on the cover was "a pretty apt description of one financial rendering inside the report." Loomis concluded that a major downsizing in 1996 "didn't lop off the part of the company, nor the employees, that grill and glaze those numbers."

Other attempts to polish earnings have more substantive consequences. A common practice in many manufacturing industries is something called trade loading or channel stuffing. This refers to shipping unwanted merchandise to distributors and wholesalers near the end of a quarter to bolster reported sales and earnings, even though the final demand for the goods isn't there. Typically, the distributors don't pay for the unwanted inventory until they resell it, so the company has to finance an extra layer of receivables, which reduces cash flow. If the goods are perishables, such as candy bars or cigarettes, they go stale in the distributors' warehouses and ultimately end up disappointing consumers. If they are high-tech microcomputer components, they may be obsoleted in the warehouse and never reach end users.

In extreme cases, the thirst for reported earnings leads companies to go from trade loading to outright fraud. A disk-drive manufacturer called Miniscribe filed for bankruptcy in 1990 after directors discovered that the company had literally been shipping bricks to distributors. Emanuel Pinez, the chief executive of another high-tech company, Centennial Technologies, went to jail in 1997 after it was discovered that he was shipping the company's personal-computer cards to the warehouses of friends and falsely booking them as sold.

Trade loading and channel stuffing make reported earnings look better than they really are the first time a company does it, but the practice makes shareholders worse off by at least the amount of the receivables financing. And the increase in financing costs is quasi-permanent because companies usually have to keep stuffing the channel quarter after quarter to prevent a subsequent drop in reported sales. Trade loading also can give rise to additional inventory shrinkage (a polite word for theft), added storage costs, and sometimes even extra capital equipment to produce the unwanted goods. What's more, companies rarely fool anyone for long. Securities analysts are attuned to trade loading and regularly check balance sheets for the telltale sign of receivables that are growing faster than sales.

Perhaps the most insidious impact of the emphasis on earnings is the way that it encourages managers to overinvest in mature industries. When the focus is purely on earnings, any investment—even one with a negative net present value—will look good to top management so long as the project's return is more than the after-tax borrowing rate on additional debt. And prospective investments will look even better at the operating level. Line managers become eager coconspirators in overinvestment because their performance appraisals (and bonuses) typically are based on operating profits alone, without even a charge for the cost of debt.

Consider a $10-million expansion that is expected to produce an 8% return, or $800,000 a year in operating profits after taxes and after depreciation. If a company's weighted average cost of capital is 10%, the $800,000 a year in operating profits has a present value of $8 million. Subtracting the $10 million investment to make the expansion yields a net present value, or NPV, of minus $2 million. Valuing the project on the basis of EVA arrives at exactly the same result. Subtracting a capital charge of $1 million (10% of the $10-million investment) from the operating profits results in an annual EVA of minus $200,000, and the present value of a negative $200,000 a year is minus $2 million. Viewed through the lens of EVA or NPV, the project will reduce the company's MVA by $2 million.

Now look at the same project in terms of its effect on earnings. The expansion looks great at the operating level, where there is no charge for debt or equity. It boosts operating profits by $800,000 a year. The project also looks good at the corporate level. Since accounting earnings treat equity as though it is free, the only added deduction at that level is the after-tax cost of debt. Assume that the company finances new investments with a mix of 70% equity and 30% debt, which is about average, and its after-tax borrowing cost is 5%, also about average in the late nineties. The after-tax interest cost on $3 million of new borrowings is just $150,000, or 1.5% of the $10-million investment. The project boosts reported earnings by $650,000 a year. The EVA and NPV tests both say this investment will destroy $2 million of shareholder wealth, but the earnings test tells management to go ahead with it. Indeed, the earnings test would tell management to go ahead with any investment with an after-tax return greater than 1.5%.

Those who manage for higher earnings are relying on what is known as the "accounting" model of stock valuation. The accounting model holds that a vague combination of earnings per share, earnings growth, and return on equity determine expected future profits and, in turn, stock prices. The main competing explanation of stock valuation is called the economic model. The economic model holds that investors care about only two things: the cash that a business can be expected to generate over its life and the riskiness of the expected cash receipts. An abundance of academic research shows that the economic model does a much better job of explaining movements in stock prices, and that the accounting model is simply wrong. The empirical evidence also shows that EVA, which is derived from the economic model, correlates much more closely with changes in MVA than any other performance measure.

Financial economists have tested the relative merits of the accounting and economic models by examining the behavior of stock prices on occasions when earnings and cash flow diverge, and have found that cash flow wins every time. One of the most telling studies was by Shyam Sunder at the University of Chicago way back in the mid-1970s. Sunder looked at the performance of stock prices when companies announced they were shifting from FIFO to LIFO inventory accounting. Under FIFO (for first in, first out) the prices used in calculating costs are those of the oldest materials in inventory; under LIFO (last in, first out), accountants use prices of the most recently purchased materials when they calculate costs. The difference becomes important in times of high inflation because FIFO uses older, lower prices and yields lower costs. That makes profits look better, but it also subjects companies to taxes on so-called inventory profits.

Most corporations used FIFO until the early seventies, when inflation soared and taxes on inventory profits shot up along with it. In 1975 alone, hundreds of large corporations made the shift to LIFO to reduce their tax bills. They did so reluctantly, however, because the SEC requires companies to use the same inventory accounting in their public reporting to shareholders as they use on their tax returns. Thus, companies fretted because the shift to LIFO, while saving a bundle in taxes, would also cause reported earnings to drop. They needn't have worried. Sunder found that the stocks of companies switching to LIFO jumped an average of 5% when they announced the change. Investors realized that LIFO would mean lower earnings per share, but they also knew that the tax savings represented a real improvement in cash flow for shareholders, and that's what mattered.

Academic studies also show that the conventional wisdom about goodwill write-offs is all wrong. Goodwill is the difference between the price paid for an acquired company and the "fair value" of its assets in transactions using the "purchase" method of accounting. Acquirers are required to write off the goodwill, and charge it against earnings, over a period of 40 years or less. Many executives, and even Wall Street analysts and investment bankers, believe the amortization of goodwill hurts the stocks of acquirers even though it is merely a bookkeeping entry that does not affect cash flow (except in cases where acquirers can take a tax deduction for part of the write-off, in which case it *helps* their cash flow).

In an extensive survey of the academic research on this subject, Michael L. Davis of Lehigh University concluded that the specter of goodwill write-offs does affect the behavior of some acquirers, and in ways that reduce shareholder wealth. Many companies apparently are willing to pay higher acquisition premiums in order to treat acquisitions as poolings of interests, an accounting treatment that does not give rise to goodwill, with the result that their stocks *underperform* the stocks of acquirers that use purchase accounting (and suffer the ignominy of goodwill amortization). In the most famous case in recent years, AT&T went to bizarre lengths to ensure that it could treat its acquisition of NCR as a pooling of interests. Economists Thomas Lys and Linda Vincent, who made a detailed study of that transaction, concluded that AT&T paid at least $500 million extra to secure pooling treatment. Davis also concluded that the goodwill that companies using the purchase method of accounting have to put on their balance sheets is reflected in their stock prices, but the subsequent write-off of goodwill is not. In other words, the stock market recognizes that goodwill has value, and that the amortization of it is a phantom expense.

Other studies put the lie to the popular myth that investors are too short-term oriented. Institutional investors, who win or lose business on the basis of their performance, are said to be especially hungry for quarterly earnings gains. The attendant pressure from the stock market, the story goes, forces corporate managers to sacrifice long-term improvements for short-term profit gains, focusing on financial engineering and deal making instead of investing in research and development projects, employee training, and other initiatives with distant payoffs. The market myopia argument is especially popular among the antitakeover crowd. Andrew Sigler, the former chairman of Champion International, a champion underperformer, frequently argued that institutional investors are opportunistic short-term traders who don't have the long-term perspective of a true owner.

A two-year study by the Council on Competitiveness and the Harvard Business School, called *Capital Choices*, also subscribed to the myopia myth. The research team, led by professor Michael Porter, concluded that excessive emphasis on short-term results was stifling investment and undermining U.S. competitiveness, and that the problem had worsened in the seventies and eighties, the decades when institutional ownership and takeovers both took off. Writing in

1992 in the *Journal of Applied Corporate Finance*, Porter bemoaned the fact that the United States lacks the "patient" capital that Germany and Japan enjoy. Unfortunately for Porter and company, the *Capital Choices* findings don't square with the increasing competitiveness of U.S. industry since the early eighties. And as noted before, the more recent McKinsey study shows that patient capital is an affliction, not an elixir.

In a response to Porter in the same issue of the *Journal of Applied Corporate Finance*, Peter L. Bernstein, the founding editor of the *Journal of Portfolio Management* and author of *Against the Gods*, argued convincingly that investors care very much about the future. For one thing, the fact that stocks yield less in dividends than bonds pay in interest is simple proof that investors are focused on *future* profits. For another, the only way to explain the fact that research-oriented companies like Merck, Eli Lilly, and Intel sell at higher earnings multiples than USX Corporation or International Paper Company is that investors are paying up for the prospect of higher future profits. If investors cared only about near-term results, all stocks would sell for essentially the same price-earnings ratios. Very little value—which shows up as a higher multiple of current earnings—would be placed on the prospect of future profit growth.

A number of empirical studies provide powerful support for those casual observations. John McConnell of Purdue University and Chris Muscarella of Southern Methodist University examined the share price reactions to 547 corporate announcements of capital spending plans and R&D programs from 1975 to 1981. If the market really were myopic, it would either ignore those announcements or knock down the prices of the companies' shares, since big expansion programs and R&D initiatives depress near-term accounting profits. In fact, McConnell and Muscarella found a statistically significant *increase* in share prices for companies announcing an increase in R&D or capital spending, and a drop in share prices of companies that said they were cutting those expenditures.

One of the most ambitious studies in this area was done by Su H.

Chan of California State University, John W. Kensinger of the University of North Texas, and John D. Martin of the University of Texas at Austin. They looked at announcements of increases in R&D spending from June 1979 to June 1985, and distinguished between announcements by high-tech and low-tech companies. Rather than go into the details of their statistics, we'll simply quote from the authors' conclusion:

> In brief, companies announcing planned increases in R&D spending saw immediate increases in their stock prices of more than 1.4% on average. Perhaps more revealing, high-tech companies announcing increases in R&D spending above their industry average tended to reap the greatest immediate rewards, while low-tech companies experienced *declines* in stock value. . . . It seems that investors are impressed when their money is spent for research in technology-intensive fields, but skeptical when a low-tech company throws more money than its competitors into the wishing well of research in a field that has already become mature. Surprised? Not if you are willing to give investors credit for strategic common sense.

Gregg A. Jarrell of the University of Rochester addressed the R&D issue as it applies to takeovers while he was chief economist at the Securities and Exchange Commission in the mid-1980s. The complaint from the business establishment was that institutional investors penalized companies for sacrificing short-term earnings to invest in R&D, and that the depressed stock prices resulting from this perverse behavior then attracted avaricious corporate raiders. As a result, institutional investors were forcing prudent managers to forego attractive research projects in order to save themselves from becoming takeover bait. What Jarrell found, however, was that the companies that had been hit with unwanted takeover bids were ones that spent *less* on R&D, expressed as a percentage of sales, than other companies in their industries. In other words, the antitakeover crowd had things backward.

Lisa Meulbroek of Harvard took the takeover analysis one step further. If managers really are scrimping on R&D because they are afraid of takeovers, she reasoned, then companies that adopt poison pills and other shark repellants should be able to take advantage of their takeover protection to invest more for the long term. But she found that R&D more often declines following the adoption of anti-takeover provisions. In other words, the protection afforded by shark repellants apparently exacerbates *management* myopia.

Even if the accounting model is flawed, why is EVA so superior? First, by charging for capital, EVA discourages managers from making investments that return less than cost of capital. Moreover, the EVA formula includes a number of adjustments to conventional accounting to correct such things as the amortization of goodwill and the immediate expensing of R&D (see Chapter 11 for a discussion of the accounting adjustments). This eliminates accounting anomalies in GAAP and makes EVA a more accurate *period-to-period* measure of wealth creation, so it can be used as a period-to-period operating goal. Equally important, EVA is the performance measure that is most directly linked to MVA. As explained in Chapter 3, a company's MVA is the present value of the amount by which investors expect future profits to exceed or fall short of the cost of capital. In other words, the "profit" that determines MVA is *economic profit*, or operating profit minus the cost of capital. That's EVA.

Thus, MVA is, by definition, the present value of expected future EVA—which means that managing for increases in EVA is the most direct way to manage for an increase in MVA. Simplistically, if a company increases its EVA and investors expect the increase to be permanent, MVA will increase by the additional EVA capitalized at the cost of capital. Nothing is so simple in the stock market, of course. In practice, an increase in EVA could cause investors to expect more increases in the future, bringing a larger increase in MVA. Or, investors may expect the change to be transitory, so that the multiplier will be smaller.

So much for theory. What about the real world? Several examples show the link between EVA and MVA quite vividly. (See Figure 5.1.) One of the most dramatic is IBM. Its EVA peaked in 1984 at $4.7 billion, and then dropped in a fairly straight line all the way to minus $204 million in 1989. IBM's MVA took a similar dive, from more than $50 billion in 1985 to close to zero in 1989. In other words, a net decline in EVA of $4.5 billion brought a decline in MVA roughly 11 times as large. EVA told what was happening at Big Blue, but earnings did not. Earnings peaked at $6.6 billion in 1985 but were still up at $5.8 billion in 1989. If the IBM board had been watching EVA instead of earnings, it might have fired John Akers several years earlier. It didn't, and the carnage continued beyond 1989. By 1992, when IBM's MVA bottomed at minus $23.7 billion and its EVA had reached minus $5.3 billion, the company had fallen all the way from No. 1 to No. 1000 on the Performance 1000.

SPX Corporation, which went on EVA at the beginning of 1996, improved its EVA by $26.6 million that year, and its MVA shot up by $348 million. The gain in MVA was so large (13 times the change in EVA) that it indicates the market anticipated, correctly as it turned out, that SPX's EVA would continue to improve.

Figure 5.1

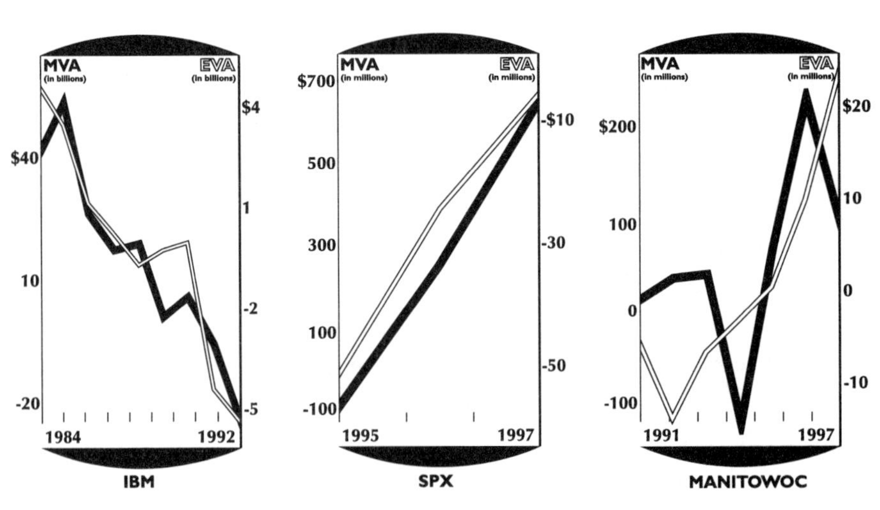

The Manitowoc Company, a once-faltering Wisconsin conglomerate that repairs ships and makes construction cranes and commercial ice machines, adopted EVA in 1992. Over the next four years, Manitowoc managed to improve its EVA by $24 million, from minus $14 million to a positive $10 million. Its MVA rose by $162 million.

Stern Stewart has done a number of empirical tests of the relationship between EVA and MVA. Using the Performance 1000 database, it finds that EVA statistically "explains" about half the movement in a company's MVA. That may not sound very impressive until you learn that no other performance measure explains nearly as much of the change in MVA. Figure 5.2 shows how the various measures stack up in terms of explaining changes in MVA.

Since stock prices are expectational, no performance measure can

Figure 5.2

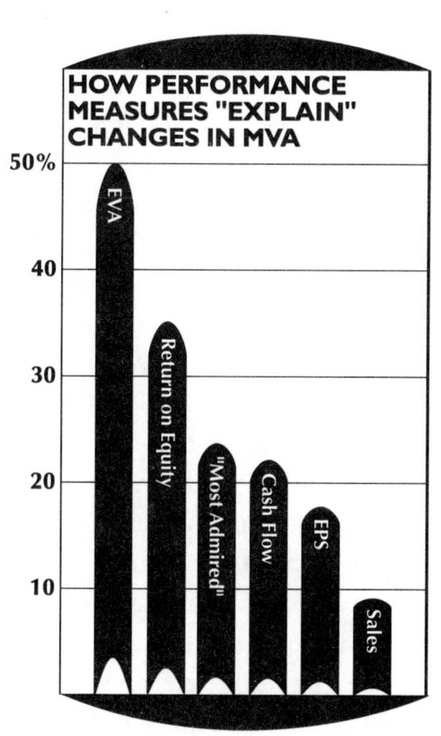

possibly correlate perfectly with changes in MVA. Current performance is the single most important thing investors look at in forming expectations, but other things—like the new drugs a pharmaceutical company has in the pipeline—also count. That partly explains why EVA explains only 50% of the changes in MVA. In addition, the Stern Stewart tests were done using standard adjustments to GAAP for all companies. The resulting EVA estimates are somewhat off the mark because EVA, as you will see later on, has to be tailored to each company. Stern Stewart has done EVA/MVA correlations for specific industries, with accounting adjustments tailored to their circumstances, and has found that in some cases EVA can explain more than 70% of the changes in MVA. The implication is that a more refined EVA calculation, like the ones EVA companies use in their internal measures, would tie even more closely to MVA. The research also shows, by the way, that each $1 increase in EVA brings, on average, a $9.50 increase in MVA.

Independent researchers, including James L. Grant of the Simmons Graduate School of Business, also have found that EVA tracks MVA better than other measures. Two researchers at the University of Pittsburgh, Kenneth Lehn, another former chief economist at the SEC, and Anil K. Makhija, discovered another interesting fact about EVA and MVA. Specifically, they found that low MVA and EVA numbers more than double the chance that the CEO will be sacked. Among the companies in their study with an MVA above the median, 8.6% had fired their CEOs. But among those with MVAs below the median, the CEO sack rate jumped to 20%. The results were similar for EVA, with CEO turnover rates of 9% when EVA was above the median and 19.3% when it was below the median. Significantly, Lehn and Makhija found no relationship between CEO turnover and return on equity or return on assets. In other words, CEOs should measure their own performance against MVA and EVA, because shareholders will do so whether they like it or not.

All the evidence about what really determines stock prices leads to an inescapable question: If the accounting model is so wrong, why does Wall Street remain fixated on quarterly earnings reports? The answer is that the smartest securities analysts and portfolio managers never have paid much attention to raw accounting data. A favorite pastime of Warren Buffett, for example, is reading annual reports and ferreting out accounting legerdemain. The best analysts and portfolio managers talk in terms not of earnings, but of earnings properly adjusted and purged of distortions. They always have had informal methods of converting accounting earnings into economic earnings. That's why the market moves with economics and not with earnings.

And just as corporations have been turning to EVA in increasing numbers in recent years, a rapidly growing contingent of analysts and money managers have been formalizing their restatements of accounting numbers by using the EVA model to value securities. At least a few of the analysts at almost every investment house use EVA in place of earnings in their valuation work. And two of the leading investment banks, Credit Suisse First Boston and Goldman Sachs, have adopted EVA firmwide as a principal basis for equity valuation. First Boston puts the case this way in its "EVA Primer":

- Earnings per share can be manipulated by accounting practices. Nor does this measure provide a clear understanding of the variables that drive value, such as operating margins, cost of capital, and competitive advantage period.
- The EVA methodology explicitly addresses business and financial risk and allows the investor to gauge the magnitude and sustainability of returns. Moreover, this structure examines the three fundamental principles of value creation: cash flow, risk, and sustainability of returns. Of all financial measures, it best explains the creation of shareholder value.

Goldman Sachs is equally clear in its explanation of EVA:

> The EVA approach to equity analysis has become increasingly popular because it more accurately reflects economic reality (as opposed to accounting reality) when compared with many traditional valuation measures, such as earnings per share (EPS), return on equity (ROE),

> and free cash flow; those accounting-based measures can be distorted by accounting practices. They also include the cost of debt and exclude the cost of equity. . . . Focusing on the variables that drive the underlying economics of a business, rather than accounting-based benchmarks, should result in improved management, financial analysis, and ultimately, enhanced shareholder value.

The buy side—the portfolio managers who actually own stocks—also has been turning to EVA. Anthony J. Kreisel, manager of the Putnam Growth and Income Fund II and comanager of the Putnam Fund for Growth and Income, says EVA has become his "most significant analytical tool." Says Kreisel: "I couldn't care less what next quarter's earnings are going to be." Scores of other "value" investors also are using EVA, including CalPERS (the California Public Employee Retirement System), the largest institutional investor in the United States. Says Bob Boldt, the senior investment officer who picked EVA as a criterion for identifying companies for CalPERS's corporate-governance focus list: "I wasn't satisfied that we were seeing [poorly performing] companies early enough. I concluded that we should look at a more direct economic measure to see how management was managing from an economic point of view, and I zeroed in on EVA as the best measure of economic performance."

6

Serving the Service Industries

Some people wrongly assume that EVA is just a tool for manufacturers, and has comparatively little to offer service companies. They mistakenly believe that EVA's emphasis on capital costs means that it doesn't really help much unless a company is laden with factories full of heavy equipment and has a small fortune tied up in raw materials and work-in-process inventories. In fact, the scores of service companies already using EVA can attest to the fact that it is just as great a tonic for them as it is for any other kind of business. Over the past half-decade, EVA has helped improve the performance of companies in retailing, telecommunications, credit reporting, database management, freight transport and logistics, trucking, industrial services, financial services, health care, and an assortment of other service areas. Successful users of EVA include W. W. Grainger in wholesale distribution; Ryder Systems in truck leasing and logistics management; Dun & Bradstreet in financial information services; Globopar, the largest media company in Brazil; ISS A/S of Denmark, the world's largest facilities cleaning company, with operations in 30 countries; and Tenet Healthcare, the second-largest for-profit hospital company in the United States.

So why the misconception? One reason is EVA's presumed emphasis on the cost of capital. This in itself is a misconception. EVA only seems to accentuate capital costs because most other performance measures totally ignore the cost of equity capital by treating shareholder funds as though they were free. In actuality, EVA puts an equal emphasis on operating costs and capital costs. What's more, EVA can provide a superior performance measure and decision tool even if a company has virtually no capital at all because the calculation of NOPAT (net operating profits after taxes) corrects the anomalies in conventional accounting earnings.

Another reason for the misconception is that many people think of service businesses as being limited to law firms, restaurants, laundries, and the like (as in, "We're becoming a nation where all we do is take in one another's laundry"). In fact, services encompass every business other than manufacturers and those that harvest or mine a natural resource, and many service businesses use far more capital than is generally appreciated. Telecommunications (see Chapter 10) is one of the most capital-intensive of all industries, using almost a dollar of capital for each dollar of revenues. Airlines, theme parks, and restaurants all use substantial amounts of capital. Just ask any McDonald's franchisee. Retailers employ prodigious amounts of capital in the form of inventories and store space. The stores typically do not show up on balance sheets because they are leased, but they represent capital just the same; in calculating EVA, leases are capitalized and included in the computation of the capital charge.

Retailing also happens to be an industry in which EVA can be especially effective, largely because most of the EVA centers—the units for which EVA is separately calculated—are already defined by the individual stores. Major retailers in the United States and Europe have begun to recognize how useful EVA can be to them. The Burton Group in the United Kingdom went on EVA in 1996, J. C. Penney began a multiyear EVA implementation in 1997, and Toys "Я" Us® decided to adopt EVA in 1998. Securities analysts realize this as well. When they raised their recommendation on Penney to a "strong buy" in January 1998, BT Alex. Brown analysts Patrick F. McCormack and Alex S. Rafal cited EVA as one of the key positives at the company. "J. C. Penney is becoming an EVA company and we think that is important," they wrote. ". . . This emphasis on return-on-capital is extremely encouraging, in our view, and we believe that retailers can benefit enormously by genuinely adopting measures such as this."

Penney decided to adopt EVA precisely because its managers had paid too little heed to capital costs. "People were unaware of the balance sheet and what really was there," says Rodney Carter, director of Penney's EVA program. "We focused on expense. So, if we needed to drive sales and profits, we would invest a lot of capital. To make people more aware of all the costs, we wanted a more inclusive measure to calculate and reflect performance." Carter adds that Penney also wanted a measure that operating employees could readily understand. "We needed to provide a common financial language that was understandable, credible, and actionable," he says. "That really was key in picking EVA." Penney put 450 of its executives on EVA incentives in 1998, with plans to add 5,000 more in 1999, and has been training its 250,000 employees at a rate of about 20,000 a year. "We want this to be a part of the company, as opposed to being just another initiative," says Carter. "It's critical in a company our size that it continue to be reinforced in the halls, in staff meetings, and in quarterly updates."

Two South African retailers have been using EVA with stunning results. The stocks of both companies more than tripled in less than three years after they put all their managers, down to the store level, on EVA incentives. One is JD Group, which includes more than half a dozen chains of furniture stores and another that sells appliances and consumer electronics. In all, JD has more than 500 stores and 11,000 employees. The company is the creation of David Sussman, a hard-driving entrepreneur who opened his first Price 'n Pride furniture store in 1983 after concluding that his career at another furniture retailer had stalled. Three years later he acquired the Joshua Doore chain (whence the JD in JD Group), the furniture chain where he had started as a receiving clerk in 1976.

Sussman decided to implement EVA in 1995 after it became clear to him that the company's returns were suffering because it wasn't taking the full picture of its business down to the store managers. "We had always left them with the responsibility of handling the traditional profit-and-loss account, but we had never exposed the balance sheet to our branch [store] managers," he says. "We tried to manage the return on capital at the top. But it became clear to us that we were not going to be as successful as we wanted to be until the branch managers became responsible for the total picture." Sussman also wanted to reduce the assets in the stores as a way to reduce leverage. JD provides financing to many of its customers, which makes it a sort of quasi-bank. That lifts its leverage much higher than most other retailers, and Sussman believed that securities analysts perceived JD as being riskier than it really was.

JD saw dramatic improvements in EVA from the very start. "In many instances," says Sussman, "our guys down the line have become more ruthless than I am in our pursuit of getting a return. We have seen an amazing change in culture coming about at the branch manager level." Mias Strauss, a deputy managing director, says the inclusion of capital costs in performance evaluations has changed attitudes from the store level up through senior management at the individual chains, each of which is a separate business unit. "Previously, a guy would make a couple hundred thousand bottom-line and thought he was doing a good job, even if the cost of capital was greater. Now what he says is, 'How much capital is involved, and is the money I'm making more than the cost of capital?' Our general managers at our business units used to be very reluctant to close a branch. They really had to lose money [on an operating basis] before they came to you and said let's close a branch. Now the business-unit managers are very keen."

One manifestation of the new attitude at the store level is a reluctance to spend money on capital equipment. In the past, JD replaced its delivery trucks on a regular schedule. The month that a truck was scheduled to be replaced, the capital-expenditure request was sure to come in to headquarters. "It was a civil-service type attitude," says Strauss. "If it's in the budget, I must use it. And it was granted." Now that they are on EVA incentives, the store managers are refurbishing trucks instead of replacing them. That has helped offset the cost of the armed guards that JD had to put on all its delivery trucks in 1996. "It's very hard to achieve world-class productivity when crime is so bad that you have to put an extra person on every truck," says Sussman.

Managers also have become much sharper at negotiating leases. Since going on EVA, about 25% of the lease renewals have been at reduced rents, sometimes as much as 50% less than the previous rates. JD also is renting smaller spaces. Store managers used to believe that more space always was better than less. Now they have a better fix on how many square meters are needed to display the range of goods without any duplication on the floor. "Some of our business units are locked into leases," says Strauss. "So they are lopping off a portion of the shop and building a drywall partition and subletting the space. That's common, and it's not a corporate decision. That's a business-unit decision and they are making those decisions without our forcing them in any way." Meanwhile, the business units have been spending *more* money on marketing and promotions. "One of the reasons we have done so well is because of the aggressiveness in marketing," says Strauss.

Sussman says the most profound change from EVA, apart from much sharper asset management, is a singular focus throughout the organization. "From the branch managers to ourselves at corporate, everyone is now talking one language," he says. "We're all looking at the whole picture. EVA is a very simple tool that everybody applies in exactly the same way. It's a management tool that senior management and middle management and branch managers can use to make decisions on a day-to-day basis, and they're all saying, 'Is this in the best interest of the business? Yes or no?' "

The New Clicks group, another major South African retailer, also adopted EVA in 1995. The company operates three retail chains: Clicks stores sell health, home, and beauty products aimed at upper-income families; Diskom sells similar products, with the exception of cosmetics, to the lower end of the market, and Musica is the market leader in popular music. New Clicks turned to EVA for two reasons. First, management felt that the old bonus system, based on performance against negotiated budgets, wasn't working. Second, Peter Green, the managing director for corporate services, wanted a way to charge individual stores for the inventories they carried as a way of compelling them to operate leaner. He wanted to get capital out of existing stores so the company could put it into new technology—for such things as tracking inventories and automatically reordering stock—and into an ambitious expansion program.

The expansion accelerated with the sale of New Clicks by the Premier group to Malbak, another South African company. Just five months later, Malbak announced the decision to unbundle its assets, including its 51% interest in New Clicks. Freed of what CEO Trevor Honneysett calls "the mould of having a big parent," Clicks grew from 353 stores in 1995 to nearly 450 at the end of 1997, and plans to have 600 across southern Africa by the year 2000.

The Clicks store managers began trimming their inventories immediately, and Green got the reductions he wanted—to the tune of one complete inventory turn in the first year alone. The store managers also began putting pressure on buyers to stop saddling them with goods that weren't selling well, something Green had encouraged the store managers to do. That caused some initial anxiety on the part of the buyers, Green says, but by the end of the first year they were working enthusiastically with store managers to improve the product selections. Store managers also are paying closer attention to how they allocate space. "It has caused people to think about things which they have always taken for granted," says Green. "You look at a sunglasses stand, for instance, and you work out the investment in merchandise on that stand and the space it occupies, and you are horrified."

Green's cohorts in the executive suite were startled at the bonuses some store managers earned in the first year under the special EVA remuneration scheme, and worried that they might be too large. "The real achievers can get quite big money," says Green. "But if you look at the performance, you have to conclude that it's deserved." Green's fellow executives came to the same conclusion, and soon were so pleased with how the bonus plan was working that they extended it to all store employees in 1997. Now, teams made up of all the employees in a store analyze operations, identify deficiencies, and formulate plans to correct them. Lower-level employees also have become more diligent about alerting managers to shoplifting, which, like the hijacking of delivery trucks, has become a severe problem in South Africa. So-called climate audits by human-resource consultants have found that morale has improved and motivation is greater throughout the stores. "Quite an important aspect of the EVA system," says Green, "is a cultural change and a sense of empowerment."

One of the first service companies to adopt EVA was Equifax Inc., the Atlanta-based credit reporting giant, which did so in 1992. Equifax touches the lives of millions of consumers in the United States and abroad when they apply for credit cards, open bank accounts, or write a check to a merchant. In 1995, for example, Equifax transmitted 385 million credit reports to its customers, did the data processing for nine million credit cards, and guaranteed a total of $15 billion in personal checks. The check-guarantee business is little known to the public. If a sales clerk accepts your check after a bit of processing behind the counter, it is likely that an Equifax computer hundreds or thousands of miles away has validated your honesty and guaranteed payment. If your check bounces, Equifax bears the loss.

Equifax grew out of an old-fashioned credit bureau in Atlanta, founded in 1899 and for decades called the Retail Credit Bureau. It expanded by acquiring other credit bureaus, first regionally and then nationally and internationally. In the late 1980s, however, the company was in the doldrums. Facing retirement, Equifax's top management looked outside for fresh talent and in 1987 imported C. B. (Jack) Rogers, Jr., a high-ranking IBM executive who was a member of Equifax's board. Rogers served as president and chief operating officer for two years and became chief executive in 1989. "When I got here," he says, "there was only one business making any money [credit reporting], there were a lot of businesses that were mediocre, and one business that was awash in significant red ink." That was the insurance business, which was highly labor-intensive. "It was clear we had to do some building."

Rogers had multiple goals: to cut fat, to automate labor-intensive operations, to expand both internationally and into new product lines, and to decentralize a top-heavy organization. But he had a problem in dispersing responsibility and decision making down the line. "We did not have a good means of measuring performance," says Rogers. That felt need sparked his interest in EVA, which he had become acquainted with as a director of Briggs & Stratton. At the same time, Derek Smith, then CFO, was getting interested in the subject through his own work on developing a comprehensive financial strategy. "The biggest issue facing us was how we were judging the basic return on capital," Smith recalls. "There was a major disconnect between operating performance and the capital being poured into the business to generate that operating performance."

EVA has benefited the company in many ways—primarily as a new method to analyze financial results and as a technique to elicit better performance from the managers at headquarters and down the line. Rogers, who stepped down as CEO at the end of 1996, crisply summarizes the superiority of EVA over other methods of motivating managers, such as linking bonuses to per-share earnings: "It is very difficult to tell a manager down the line, 'Harry, we're going to measure you on EPS.' Harry doesn't have a clue as to how he can help EPS, particularly if he has a small business unit and he knows that the guys in credit reporting are carrying much of the water."

By contrast, says Rogers, "EVA seemed to have an answer where everybody could play. Now you could say, 'Harry, we're going to measure you on the wise use of capital, on how well you deploy these capital assets.' " To reinforce that message, Rogers instituted the practice of separating the heads of Equifax's business units into two groups at their monthly meetings—value creators and value destroyers. "You don't want to be a value destroyer," says Rogers. "It's a terrible term, but that's what you're doing. If your money costs you 12% and you're returning 6%, don't tell me you're making money."

The spotlight on capital revolutionized the way the company conducted its business. It also transformed Equifax's balance sheet. In all the years since 1899, the company had never issued any public debt. Its steady expansion over the decades had been financed out of equity and retained earnings, with bank lines providing any needs for short-term financing. Smith attributes the company's disdain for debt to the inherent conservatism of a company that passed judgment on the probity of others. Low debt was a mark of soundness, not to say virtue. And since the company was not capital-intensive and had substantial cash flow, it had no great need of long-term debt. But equity costs a lot more than debt; Equifax's cost of capital in 1992 was a sky-high 13%.

That fall the company pared its cost of capital—and boosted its EVA—by issuing $200 million of bonds at an interest rate of 6.5%, which came to under 4% after taxes. Equifax used the proceeds to repurchase stock. "The implementation of an EVA-based financial strategy lent strong support and credibility to Equifax's adoption of EVA financial management practices and incentives," says Dennis Soter, a Stern Stewart partner who advised the company on the leveraged recapitalization. "But the dramatic rise in stock price that followed the $200-million buyback far exceeded the increase predicted by EVA alone. The new financial strategy was viewed by investors as supportive of EVA and evidence of management's commitment to running the company for the benefit of its stockholders."

The leveraged recap was so successful that the company spent another $100 million in open-market share repurchases in 1994 and 1995. It also decided to gradually reduce its dividend payout ratio, which had been greater than 50% of earnings, to 30%. The lowered dividend payout ratio helped provide the funds for an additional $200 million of share repurchases that the board authorized in the second half of 1995.

Meanwhile, Equifax's managers began focusing on the capital tied up in operations. One of the most dramatic improvements came in accounts receivable. "We have a huge amount of our capital base stored in our receivables," says Smith. Like all companies, Equifax repeatedly urged business units to speed up their collections, but it had never given them a clear incentive to do so. But once a capital charge on receivables was added to the measure of operating performance, the business units were motivated to send out bills more promptly and get on the phone to slow payers. Prior to EVA, receivables averaged 60 to 63 days, and Rogers recalls one business unit that averaged 120 days. The average quickly dropped to 55 days, saving the company $23 million in capital costs in its first three years on EVA.

Outsourcing has been another font of saving. In a business that does not manufacture anything but information, Equifax's capital plant had basically been its computers. With the arrival of EVA, the company began to analyze the utility of retaining its in-house capability. Doing so could ensure quality control, but only at the cost of continual capital outlays to stay ahead of swift obsolescence. The alternative was to sell the equipment and outsource to IBM's Integrated Systems Solution Technology, which Equifax did in 1993. The company signed a $700-million 10-year contract that will reduce its costs by an estimated $78 million. It might appear that Equifax has outsourced the heart of its business, but the company's crown jewels are its software, not the computers. The secrets of the software remain locked in the corporate vaults. EVA also brought a $60-million sale-leaseback of Equifax's Atlanta headquarters building and an adjacent vacant lot. The property is prime Atlanta real estate, but Rogers concluded that Equifax shouldn't be in the real estate business. Nor does the company print its own report forms, manicure its own lawns, or post its own security guards, as it once did.

The biggest change at Equifax came at the end of 1996 when the company decided to spin off its insurance service businesses into a new company called ChoicePoint Inc. The insurance group—which provides automated underwriting and risk-management information to insurance companies, corporations, and government agencies—had rid itself of red ink, but had moved away from Equifax's financial services group in terms of customers, products, and strategy. Daniel McGlaughlin, who succeeded Rogers as CEO, saw the spin-off as "an opportunity to establish more focused, swifter companies" that would be better positioned to pursue opportunities in their marketplaces without competing for corporate resources. Derek Smith, who had been running insurance services for several years, became president and CEO of the new company, while Thomas Chapman, head of financial services, succeeded McGlaughlin as CEO of Equifax at the end of 1997. While not strictly an EVA action, the spin-off was consistent with the EVA philosophy of keeping a tight operational focus.

Equifax has been so pleased with EVA that it became the first company to publish a detailed EVA calculation in its annual report. And it did so in its report for 1995, a year when its EVA declined from $21.6 million to $14.1 million (because of increases in both the cost of capital and the amount of capital employed). The setback was only temporary. By 1997 Equifax's EVA was $59.8 million, up from a minus $11.2 million in 1993. (See Figure 6.1.)

Figure 6.1

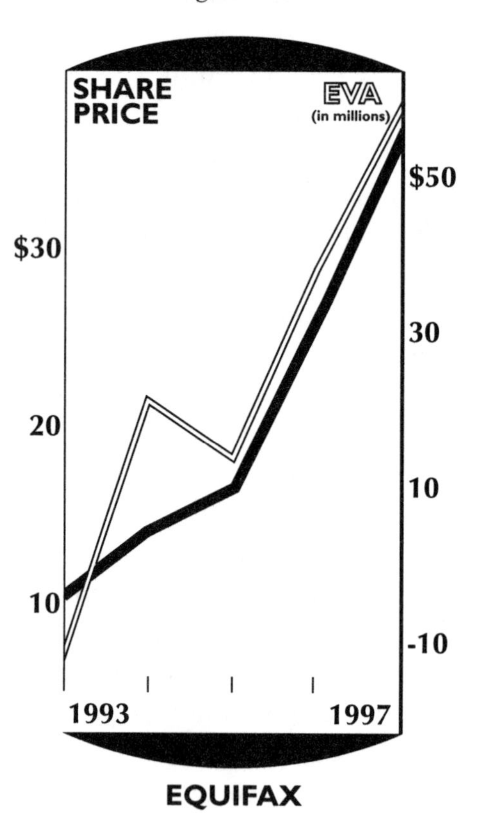

EQUIFAX

Equifax shareholders have reason to be pleased with EVA as well. In the first five years after Equifax adopted EVA, their total returns averaged 33% a year. And that excludes the gains on ChoicePoint after Equifax distributed its shares to them in the spin-off. ChoicePoint's price rose more than 50% in the first nine months after the spin-off was completed in July 1997.

7

Making Managers into Owners

The real key to the success of the EVA framework lies in using improvements in EVA in a unique type of incentive compensation plan that fires the imagination and initiative of managers and workers. Of all the variables within the control of top management and the board of directors, the one with the greatest impact on the success or failure of any enterprise is the system of rewards and incentives that shapes and directs the behavior of employees. Once you separate out all the uncontrollables—the state of the economy, the quality of the competition, and the like—nothing matters nearly so much as the diligence, enthusiasm, and creativity that a company's people bring to their work each day. People are the one factor of production, to use the economist's term, that animates all the others. Whatever value a company creates is a function of the way its people apply their energy and ideas to capital and raw materials to create goods and services that others want. And how people do their jobs is determined by the way you treat them and pay them.

Which means that accurately measuring EVA and making it the focal point of planning and analysis are not enough. When you measure performance one way but pay people on some other basis, most people will bow politely in the direction of the performance measure and march in the direction rewarded by the incentive system. "You have to align decisions with EVA," says Randall Tobias, the CEO of Eli Lilly, which adopted EVA and EVA incentives in 1994. "EVA is a very sophisticated financial tool, but it is important to understand that it is really a tool to change behavior. Linking bonuses to EVA is meant to change the whole culture." However, basing incentives on increases in EVA is just a small part of the change that is needed. Companies also have to make radical alterations in the basic design of their incentive compensation plans.

The purpose of incentives, of course, is to spur employees to work harder and smarter in order to maximize the performance of the organization. But the incentive plans used by the vast majority of companies today really are brakes on performance, and powerful twin-piston disk brakes at that. They cause managers to be much more conservative than shareholders would prefer, and often encourage them to engage in outright wealth-destroying behavior. They rob managers of initiative and motivation by paying them too little for outstanding performance and too much for poor performance. They encourage managers to game the system by negotiating easily achievable profit plans that typically fall far short of potential achievement. Then they give managers a further incentive to minimize performance whenever it is clear that the year's results are going to be above or below a narrow range around the unambitious profit goals. Substituting an EVA target for accounting-based targets in a conventional incentive plan will actually make matters worse because it creates another dimension—capital spending—in which to game the system. That is, it will encourage managers to *under*spend capital to boost short-term EVA at the expense of long-term performance.

A truly effective incentive system is one that solidly aligns the financial interest of employees with that of shareholders, improves motivation and morale, and creates an atmosphere in which managers constantly strive to create more wealth. In other words, it's an incentive system that makes managers think like and act like owners of the portions of the business they influence most directly. Stern Stewart's EVA bonus plans do just that by paying managers like owners. (Throughout this book, "EVA bonus plans" refer to ones designed by Stern Stewart, which differ dramatically from plans by other consultants.)

EVA bonus plans effectively give managers an ownership interest in performance improvements by paying bonuses that are a fixed percentage of *all* changes in EVA. They give managers the opportunity to earn an unlimited upside bonus in exchange for facing genuine downside risk. The absence of bonus caps is made possible by holding back part of the bonus earned in very good years and making it subject to loss if EVA subsequently falls. This "banking" feature—genuinely having something at risk—is what transforms managers into owners. It also minimizes the opportunities for gaming the system by ensuring that companies pay only for sustained increases in performance, and it stretches out a manager's horizon, obviating the need for a separate long-term incentive plan.

To see why EVA bonus plans are so much more effective than anything else in use today, it first helps to have a clear understanding of the dynamics of incentives and the reasons why conventional plans fail. Compensation plans typically have four key objectives:

1. To align management and shareholder interests by giving managers the motivation to choose strategies and make operating decisions that maximize shareholder wealth.
2. To provide sufficient leverage, as measured by the variability of potential rewards, to motivate managers to work long hours, take risks, and make unpleasant decisions such as laying off staff or closing a plant.
3. To limit retention risk, or the risk that valued managers will bolt for a better offer, especially during industry downturns and recessions.
4. To keep shareholder costs at a reasonable level.

Alignment and leverage are intended to deal with problems that financial economists call agency costs. That is, both reflect the fact that while all individuals want to succeed, they want other things as well, so that some extra inducement is needed to keep them focused on maximizing the performance of the firm. This is not an indictment of managers, but simply an acknowledgement of human nature. As Fred Schwed, Jr., put the matter nearly 60 years ago in *Where Are the Customers' Yachts?*, a wonderfully wry treatise on the workings of Wall Street:

> Most businessmen imagine that they are in business to make money, and that this is their chief reason for being in business, but more often than not they are gently kidding themselves. There are so many other things which are actually more attractive. Some of them are: to make a fine product or to render a remarkable service, to give employment, to revolutionize an industry, to make oneself famous, or at least to supply oneself with material for conversation in the evening. I have observed businessmen whose chief preoccupation was to try to prove conclusively to their competitors that they themselves were smart and that their competitors were damn fools—an effort which gives a certain amount of mental satisfaction but no money at all.

Balancing the four basic compensation objectives entails difficult trade-offs. A plan with extremely high leverage, for example, may pack huge incentive power, but leverage also increases the risk that valued employees will leave for a better offer in bad years. High leverage combined with poor alignment can bring unacceptably high costs as the company rewards "achievements" that do not contribute to shareholder wealth. Alternatively, for a plan to achieve both low retention risk (not much downside) and low shareholder cost (not much upside), it will necessarily have so little leverage that executives are sure to busy themselves with more attractive pursuits like the ones Schwed described.

So where do conventional incentive plans go wrong? Just about everywhere. The most obvious failing is in alignment. Using the wrong performance measure in the bonus plan guarantees that a company will get the wrong behavior. The latest incentive compensation survey by the Conference Board shows that the vast majority of corporations base their bonus payments to top corporate management on achieving targeted levels of earnings, earnings per share, operating profits, return on equity (ROE), or return on assets (ROA). Bonuses for business-unit managers usually are determined largely by the performance of the business unit itself, measured in either after-tax earnings or operating profits, with some additional weighting for overall corporate results. The alignment in these plans is unacceptably feeble because, as we saw in Chapter 5 and will see in more detail later on, the various permutations of accounting profits are not systematically linked to shareholder value. Among other things, earnings make no provision for the opportunity cost of equity capital and the impact of balance-sheet management on the true bottom line, with the result that some actions that increase accounting earnings actually destroy shareholder wealth.

Measures such as ROE and ROA are just as bad as earnings even though they do take the balance sheet into account. Since both the numerator (earnings) and the denominators (shareholders' equity or assets) are distorted by accounting anomalies, there is no reason to expect that a ratio of the two will convey any meaning at all. ROE suffers from the added shortcoming of being easily manipulated; so long as the return on assets exceeds the after-tax cost of debt, top management can boost ROE at will simply by issuing bonds and repurchasing stock. Paying the heads of business units for increases in ROA actually can create the worst of all worlds. A division head whose ROA is, say, 25% will turn down proposed investments that promise anything less, even if they will return more than the cost of capital and would add to shareholder wealth. But heads of divisions with an ROA of 5% will try to spend their way out of trouble by accepting just about any investment. They will be better off even if an investment returns less than the cost of capital and destroys shareholder wealth.

The corporate governance movement has made boards of directors acutely sensitive to the feeble connection between executive compensation and shareholder value. Research by Harvard professor Michael Jensen and others has demonstrated that the cash compensation paid to top management is largely unaffected by performance; the CEO makes out handsomely regardless of how shareholders fare. Boards have responded to those findings—and to the rampant political and press criticism of escalating CEO compensation—by supplementing chief executive pay packages with stock options, lots of stock options. Notice that the operative word here is supplement, not replace. Cash compensation has continued to rise, and remains remarkably insensitive to performance.

The goal of options, of course, is to improve the alignment between CEO pay and shareholder interests, and boards have succeeded at doing that. Research by Brian J. Hall and Jeffrey B. Liebman of Harvard has found that when changes in the value of stock and stock options are included in the calculations, total CEO pay became six to eight times more sensitive to changes in stock-market performance between 1980 and 1994. Nearly all of the increase in sensitivity came from much greater grants of options and restricted stock. As Hall and Liebman put it, "Sensitivity based on changes in salary and bonus [in response to stock-market performance] . . . are essentially in the rounding error of changes in the value of stock and stock options." Better alignment is no surprise given the huge increase in option awards. Hall and Liebman found that back in 1980 only 57% of the CEOs of companies on the *Forbes* 500 held any options at all, and just 30% received option grants that year. By 1994, 87% of the CEOs had options and 70% got new awards that year. The median CEO received no option award at all in 1980, while his 1994 counterpart got an award with a value of $325,000 (based on the Black-Scholes option-pricing model). Meanwhile, the median salary and bonus rose from $567,000 to $1,050,000 (in constant 1994 dollars) over those same years.

Options are an effective way to achieve alignment between the interests of CEOs and shareholders, but their usefulness (other than as a tax-effective method of compensation) rapidly diminishes as you move down through the executive ranks. To be sure, share ownership or stock options can give employees a greater sense of belonging, a feeling that they are part of a community instead of just a hired hand. Silicon Valley companies are famous for granting options to everyone, and several EVA companies, including Monsanto and Guidant Corporation, have done the same thing with great effect. But options are not very effective at motivating specific types of behavior.

For one thing, a middle manager has an exceedingly difficult time seeing the connection between his or her individual performance and the value of the company's stock. While the value of the stock ultimately represents the accumulation of the individual performances of everyone within the organization, the contribution of any one person, even the head of a business unit, usually is an imperceptible part of the whole. Stock ownership is simply too abstract and too remote to have a strong influence on behavior. This makes options extremely susceptible to what economists call the free-rider problem—sitting back and letting everyone else take care of the stock price—and emasculates their power as an incentive.

What's more, the type of options granted by most corporations are an unnecessarily expensive way of achieving alignment even for the CEO. With comparatively few exceptions, boards of directors bestow options that have a life of 10 years and an exercise price that is fixed at the market price on the day they are granted. Since the exercise price is fixed, option holders profit from *any* increase in the stock price, even one that is too small to provide shareholders with a minimally acceptable return on their investment. That is, conventional options begin rewarding managers long before the managers create any wealth for shareholders.

The solution to this disconnect between rewards and performance is to grant options with an exercise price that rises each year in line with the cost of equity capital, an alternative advocated by compensation guru Graef Crystal and others. The rising exercise price ensures that managers do not profit unless shareholders also make out decently. G. Bennett Stewart III was among the first to suggest this approach, and Stern Stewart has designed a special variety of this type of option plan for several EVA companies, including Briggs & Stratton, R. P. Scherer, and Centura Banks. Under the EVA leveraged stock option (or LSO) plans, the exercise price rises at a rate equal to the cost of equity capital minus the dividend yield and minus a modest adjustment for the inability of managers to diversify their risk. The number of options an executive gets each year is determined by the size of his or her EVA bonus. In effect, the manager uses a portion of the cash bonus to "buy" the options, though they are accounted for as a grant to avoid any immediate tax liability. By enabling managers to buy a greater number of LSO shares than they would get in a conventional option plan, the plans can be structured so that managers receive as large a dollar profit as they would reap with conventional options, but the rising strike price ensures that they win only when the shareholders win as well. Linking the option awards to the EVA bonus also makes the option grant itself a portion of variable pay and increases the leverage in the overall incentive plan.

Of the four essential compensation objectives, the only one that conventional incentive plans achieve with consistency is low retention risk, and many botch even that by paying too little to executives who perform exceptionally well. The dominant compensation strategy today is what is often called a competitive pay plan. Under this type of plan, a company sets its target compensation levels at a given percentile within its industry in order to attract and retain the caliber of executives it wants. It then assembles a compensation package typically containing base pay, a target cash bonus, and a stock option grant. If the target bonus and option package comprise 30% or more of the total, which is not uncommon, it appears that a substantial portion of the executive's pay is at risk, and that the plan delivers a large quotient of leverage.

Not so. First, consider the dynamics of the cash bonus. Target bonuses typically are paid if the executive achieves a budgeted profit plan that is negotiated annually. (We'll get back to the problems of negotiated profit plans shortly.) The Conference Board's survey of incentive practices shows that managers, on average, get no bonus at all unless they achieve at least 80% of the profit plan. If they do hit 80% of budget, they get half the target bonus. The bonus payment rises in step with profits, reaching 100% of target at 100% of the budgeted profit, and tops out at 150% of the target bonus when profits hit 120% of budget. The executive gets no incremental bonus if profit goes above 120% of budget, and the bonus is zero at anything below 80% of budget.

Conventional wisdom in the compensation arena is that this type of plan handily balances the objectives of adequate leverage and acceptable shareholder cost. As the Conference Board stated in its latest report on incentive practices: "This type of plan often is very attractive to shareholders, as both a minimum performance level and a maximum payment are established." Baloney. Such plans do have enormous leverage, but only at the single point at which profits reach 80% of plan and the bonus jumps from zero to 50% of the target level. You can be sure that no manager will ever end a year at 79% of budgeted profit.

As you can see from Figure 7.1, this type of cash bonus serves as an incentive only along a narrow segment of the spectrum of possible outcomes. Once a manager knows that the year's profit is certain to be less than 80% or more than 120% of budget—which often is clear before the fiscal year is half over—he or she no longer has a monetary incentive to maximize performance in the current year. The manager gets no extra reward for turning a good year into a great one, and faces no extra penalty for allowing a bad year to become even worse. Charles Kantor, a Stern Stewart vice

Figure 7.1

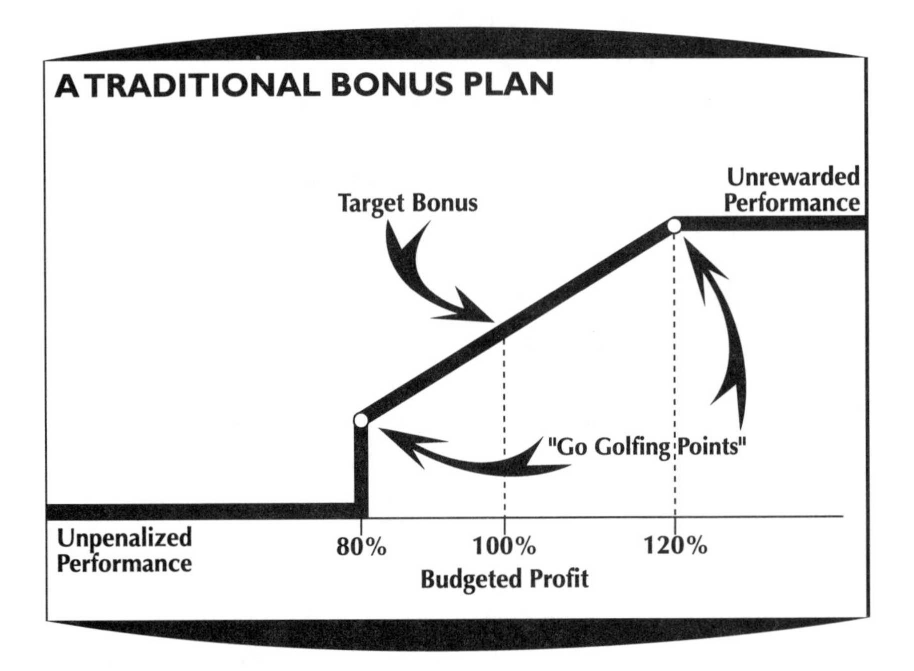

president, has quite aptly dubbed the cutoffs in conventional bonus plans the "go golfing" points, since the manager can then head for the links secure in the knowledge that slacking off won't affect the bonus.

In fact, outside the 80% and 120% cutoff points, the real incentive is to *minimize* performance at the margin. If the year is a bad one, a manager might as well let it become very bad, since that is likely to result in an easier profit plan next year. The only economic incentive working in the shareholders' interest on the nether side of the go-golfing points is managers' fear of letting performance become so terrible that it jeopardizes their chances for promotion or, at the extreme, survival with the company. If it is a good year, on the other hand, managers want to make sure it isn't too good. Performance that is way over budgeted profit will undermine their credibility when it comes time to negotiate next year's profit plan, and could cause the corporate office to raise the bar to an uncomfortably high level. Several years ago, for example, the president of a multibillion-dollar division of a *FORTUNE* 100 company instructed the business-unit heads reporting to him to suppress profits as much as possible because they were running too far ahead of the 12% growth he had promised to the CEO. He issued that order in April, less than a third of the way into the year and just two weeks before the CEO went to the annual meeting to tell shareholders how hard everyone was working on their behalf.

Some companies eliminate formal bonus caps, but not necessarily in ways that serve shareholders. One major U.S. corporation offers senior executives employment contracts with a choice of bonus plans—either a guaranteed minimum bonus of $100,000 a year or more, or a purely discretionary bonus that is set by the CEO. The message embedded in the choices is clear: Take the guaranteed minimum and that's about all you'll ever get, but cast your lot with the big guy and he will reward your show of faith by seeing to it that you always (short of being fired) get much, much more than the guaranteed minimum. Company lore has it that no one has ever opted for the guaranteed bonus. If you think these executives worry a lot about how their actions will affect shareholders, guess again.

The genuine leverage in competitive pay plans is even less than the preceding analysis suggests. Under a competitive pay strategy, companies recalibrate bonuses and option awards each year so that the total value of the package remains at the same "competitive" level and minimizes both retention risk and shareholder cost. This means that a manager starts each year with the same expected compensation (abstracting, that is, from the general upward trend in pay levels). As a result, very little of the executive's *wealth*, as represented by the present value of expected compensation over the course of his or her remaining career with the company, ever is at risk. All the manager really stands to lose—or gain—is a portion of this year's bonus payment.

It is worth noting a particularly perverse way that competitive pay plans twist option grants. Say a company does phenomenally well this year and the stock price doubles. Under a competitive pay plan in which the company keeps the *value* of option grants constant—and not the number—a manager's option grant next year will be for half as many shares. That keeps the Black-Scholes value of the option grant at the same level and keeps the total package "competitive." What this means is that stellar performance results in the manager getting half as many options, representing half as large a percentage interest in the company, as he or she was getting before. On the other hand, if the stock price drops 50%, the manager gets options on twice as many shares. Shareholder wealth doubles or drops by half, yet management's wealth hardly moves at all. What's more, the proportion of the business that shareholders give management as a reward moves in the opposite direction from that of performance.

The ubiquitous practice of negotiating annual performance targets undermines leverage even further and virtually destroys alignment. Smart managers quickly learn that the name of the game is to beat the budget, and they behave accordingly. They try to ensure that they will get the biggest possible bonus payoff by negotiating the most comfortable budget they can sell to their superiors. To them, the best plan is the most easily achievable one. And since most bonus plans place the greatest weight on producing higher operating earnings—which companies usually calculate without a charge for interest on debt or depreciation of capital equipment, let alone the cost of equity—managers are encouraged to spend capital like drunken sailors. The easiest way in the world to grow earnings is to overinvest in a mature industry. Earnings go up, but not by enough to cover the added capital, and EVA and wealth go down. To top it off, the practice of renegotiating performance targets annually encourages the shortest of short-term thinking.

The bonus negotiations, known euphemistically as the annual planning process, become unnecessarily protracted, tying up valuable time and energy as managers try to manage the expectations of their superiors instead of the business itself. The superiors, knowing full well that subordinates are trying to sandbag them, waste their time trying to control opportunism. "Our planning process before EVA amounted to collective bargaining for executive compensation," says Brian Walker, the CFO of Herman Miller. And all of this usually goes on without any explicit consideration of how the resulting plan will affect shareholder wealth.

At bottom, the effect of conventional incentive plans is to produce managers who think and act like creditors, not like owners, because their claims on the company are essentially fixed, just like those of a lender. The value of the future stream of salary, bonus, and options varies so little from year to year that it looks very much like an interest payment on debt. Since the manager has so little to gain from greater success and so much to lose if the company or division fails, his or her focus instinctively goes to the risk side of risky opportunities, not the opportunity side. Throw in the perverse incentives to game the system and sell superiors on easy goals, and one has to conclude that conventional incentive plans are formulas for mediocrity that impede rather than impel performance.

EVA bonus plans do just the opposite. By using EVA as the measure of performance, they solidly align management goals with the creation of shareholder wealth. An unlimited upside potential gives managers a continuous incentive for continuous improvement—an uncapped monetary motivation to identify and successfully carry out actions that create additional wealth. The use of a bonus bank, with a portion of exceptional bonuses held hostage and subject to loss if performance subsequently falls, causes managers to focus on projects that create enduring value. Another essential feature of these bonus plans is that targets for EVA improvement are automatically reset by a formula, which eliminates the gamesmanship created by annual negotiations. The combination of the bonus bank and the automatic resetting of target improvement has the effect of extending a manager's planning horizon and encouraging him or her to evaluate investments in terms of their impact on EVA—and bonuses—not just this year but in future years as well.

These features work together to create two characteristics of EVA bonus plans that are crucial to their effectiveness as a corporate governance mechanism: Managers know that the only way they can make themselves better off is by creating more wealth for shareholders, and they also know that they will share in any wealth they do create. This dynamic pulls management performance in the desired direction instead of requiring the constant push of exhortation from above. Some boards of directors—and most compensation consultants—miss this point, and fear that unlimited bonuses could result in unacceptably high shareholder cost. What they overlook is that extraordinary bonuses come only with extraordinary increases in EVA and, as a result, correspondingly high returns to shareholders. Managers at Armstrong World Industries, for example, received bonuses that were 2.25 times target levels for their performance in 1995. The company's stock price jumped more than 60% that year. Herman Miller's managers got bonus multiples of nearly five in fiscal 1997 and more than five in fiscal 1998, the two-year period in which Miller's stock price quadrupled.

The essential goals of the EVA bonus system, which build on the four fundamental compensation objectives previously discussed, are:

- To link performance incentives more closely to increases in shareholder wealth.
- To provide a single focus for operations management, capital budgeting, planning, performance measurement, and incentive compensation.
- To promote a culture of high performance and ownership by management, in which managers take the initiative to create value.

Bonus plans based on the EVA concept—awarding management an unlimited share of the profits remaining after providing a minimum return to shareholders—aren't new. More than 75 years ago, General Motors adopted a bonus plan that gave managers 10% of all profits in excess of a 7% return on capital. That is, GM subtracted a capital charge from after-tax profits equal to 7% of assets, and 10% of the remaining sum went into a pool to cover payouts to all employees who were eligible for bonuses. The plan, which GM used from 1922 to 1947 (GM dropped it when it began awarding stock options), represented a simple though rather elegant bargain between managers and owners: Management got 10% and shareholders got 90% of all profits that remained after deducting a salary for management and a minimum return for shareholders. The board of the Walt Disney Company crafted a similar plan for Michael Eisner when it hired him to be CEO in 1984. Under his original contract, Eisner got a bonus equal to 2% of net income in excess of a 9% return on equity. That bonus plan alone paid Eisner more than $10 million in some years, but shareholders hardly had cause to complain. In Eisner's first five years as CEO, Disney's MVA grew by $11 billion, and by the end of 1996 it had grown by nearly $29 billion.

Both the GM and Disney plans went a long way toward solving the incentive problem, but they shared several shortcomings (apart from the fact that they used conventional accounting earnings). First, a fixed share of EVA provides no incentive if a company is earning substantially less than its cost of capital, since it is a share of zero. If a company has positive EVA in some years but negative EVA at other points in the business cycle, the plan simply gives managers an option on the good years, and leaves the lower go-golfing point in place. And if a company already has highly positive EVA, management's share of the existing EVA guarantees it a large bonus no matter what happens. In effect, the board is paying the CEO as a .300 hitter simply because he was born on third base. The key elements in Stern Stewart's EVA bonus plans solve those problems, and all the other problems with conventional bonus plans. Those elements are:

- Pay for increasing EVA
- No thresholds or caps
- A target bonus
- A bonus bank
- Performance targets set by formula instead of negotiation

Pay for increasing EVA. This is the most reliable way to link the size of the bonus to the amount of wealth that management creates for shareholders, and is a precondition of making managers think and act like owners. But what is even more appealing to the people who participate in the bonus plan is that it provides them with all the right incentives at the margin, and in a way they find easy to understand. To raise EVA, managers will cut wasteful costs and raise profit without raising any more capital; they will convert nonproductive assets to cash that can be reinvested or distributed to shareholders; they will invest capital to fuel profitable growth; and they will select financial strategies that minimize the cost of capital. No other bonus plan can send such powerful messages so succinctly and accurately.

The particular EVA that determines the bonus varies with the manager in question. For the CEO and other top corporate officers, the consolidated EVA of the company is the appropriate measure. Operating managers, on the other hand, should be gauged largely or entirely by the EVA performance of their particular areas of responsibility. As a general rule, companies should try to keep measures of EVA for bonus purposes focused as tightly as possible on areas where employees have a clear line of sight and can affect outcomes through their individual actions.

No thresholds or caps. EVA plans have no go-golfing points. Managers get an unlimited share of EVA improvement, but bonuses can also be negative. (See Figure 7.2.)

Figure 7.2

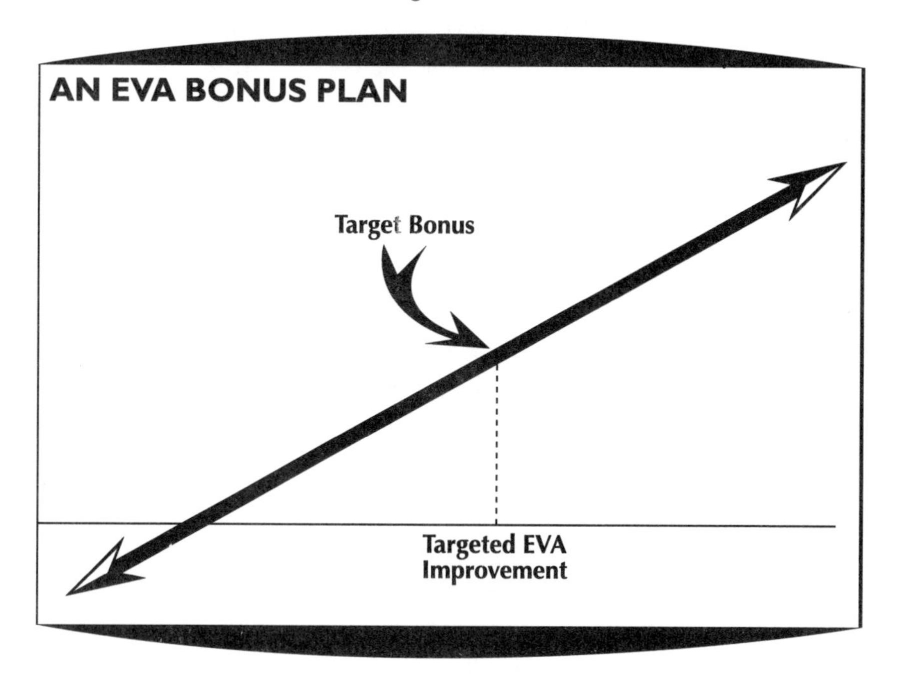

A target bonus. This is a competitive bonus based on peer company compensation practices. For two reasons, however, an EVA target bonus is larger than a conventional target bonus. First, real incentives require more leverage. Most companies put too much of a manager's compensation in the fixed portion of the pay package and too little in the variable portion. In the Conference Board survey, for example, bonuses ranged from an average of 15% of base pay for the lowest-ranking employees in the plans to just 42% of base pay for the core group of top decision makers. Second, EVA target bonuses should be higher because the potential for negative bonuses makes EVA plans inherently riskier.

A bonus bank. There are several variations as to how the bonus bank works, but the intent is always to filter large bonus swings and to defer the impact until it can be ascertained that the bonuses are associated with permanent changes in shareholder wealth. In one version of the banking system, bonuses that are deemed to fall within an acceptable range, say from zero bonus up to two times a target bonus award, are paid out each year. However, negative bonuses are withdrawn from and exceptional positive bonuses are deposited in the individual's notional bank account, and then a portion, say one-third, of any net positive bank balance in the account is also paid out each year. The unpaid balance in the bank is carried forward and the same procedure is repeated in subsequent years.

It is difficult to overemphasize the importance of the bonus bank, which performs a number of vital functions. First, it ensures that managers collect bonuses for only sustained improvements in EVA. Bonus banking also is the principal mechanism for lengthening the planning horizons of managers, since they know that gunning short-term performance won't do them any good if it harms longer-term results. Here's how Randall Tobias explained Eli Lilly's bonus bank to *FORTUNE* magazine a couple of years ago (Lilly's share price, by the way, more than doubled in the first two years after it adopted EVA):

> One of the things you never want to set up is a system where there's a great incentive to do something stupid in the short term. Theoretically you could lower your asset base and improve EVA by depleting all your inventory. . . . We've set up something called a bonus bank that encourages managers to take a longer-term perspective. The bank, in effect, acts as a longer-term scorekeeper. If a decision a manager makes today boosts EVA three years from now, the bank will reward him for it. But if the decision hurts EVA, the bank will ultimately cut his reward.

Banking also smooths out bonus payments, which can be especially helpful in limiting retention risk in highly cyclical industries. In those cases, managers build up hefty bank balances in good years and draw down on them in the poor years, as Boise Cascade did in 1995 and 1996. Finally, the bonus bank acts as a set of golden handcuffs for highly successful managers because any uncollected bank balance is forfeited if a manager resigns.

Performance targets set by formula instead of negotiation. Managers earn their target bonus when the dollar increase in EVA is equal to expected improvement. This is similar to the performance targets in conventional plans, but with two crucial differences. First, the annual amount of expected improvement typically is preset for periods of five years or so instead of being negotiated annually. Second, the base to which expected improvement is added is automatically reset up or down each year in line with actual experience.

The simplest bonus formula says that the EVA target is the EVA generated in the prior year. That means that if EVA is just maintained at its current level, the managers will earn a target bonus award each year. This is not as unreasonable as it might appear, because EVA may not be growing even though the business is. Sales, earnings, and assets may all be expanding, but profit is expanding just fast enough to provide investors with the total return they are seeking on any new capital they put into the business, and that is not bad. If EVA rises, on the other hand, that is good, and the managers will qualify for an exceptionally good bonus. By doing so they also force the EVA target to be reset that much higher for the next year without argument or debate. Even with this simple formula, the only way managers can continuously qualify for exceptional bonuses would be to continuously increase EVA.

This simple formula can work reasonably well in mature businesses where rapid expansion of EVA is unlikely. But in most industries the market (and management) expects a sustained expansion in EVA, either because the fundamentals of the business are strong (such as pharmaceuticals or soft drinks) or because the industry is turning around and rapidly consolidating (such as banks and auto suppliers). Occasionally the market is expecting EVA to deteriorate, as when drug patents are expiring. In these situations the formula for resetting the EVA target must incorporate the expected improvement or deterioration in EVA; otherwise, managers will be unfairly paid or penalized for EVA movements that are expected and already impounded in stock prices.

Stern Stewart has developed highly sophisticated, and highly proprietary, ways of calculating the amount of expected EVA improvement already incorporated in the value of a company. Suffice it to say here that for a public company, expected EVA improvement at the corporate level is based heavily, though not entirely, on a calculation of the expected future improvement implicit in the stock price, with an appropriate amortization schedule for metering the dollar amount of total improvement into each year's EVA. Other factors, which obviously become the predominant ones when calculating expected EVA improvement for private companies and for separate business units within a public company, are management forecasts, historical EVA improvement, the historical volatility of performance, and analyses of publicly owned peer companies.

Properly calibrating all the parameters in an EVA bonus plan obviously is a complex task. But the plans themselves are surprisingly simple for participants to understand, even if they have never seen a valuation model and don't have a clue what expected improvement is about. In many cases it is as simple as telling participants that their current EVA is A and that if they raise it by B to reach a target of C, they will get a target bonus of D. Moreover, the bonus will expand or contract by X percent of the amount by which EVA exceeds or falls short of C. Each participant then gets a monthly operating statement showing EVA for the month and the year to date so that one can calculate precisely the bonus earned thus far and how much one is ahead of (or behind) schedule for the year. And while bonus banks may sound complicated, most people figure them out in a matter of minutes.

One of the most important effects of EVA bonus plans is to remove incentive compensation from the annual profit planning process. Planning suddenly progresses much faster, and managers start proposing new ways to improve performance instead of trying to manage down their bosses' expectations. The result is budgets that are driven by aggressive strategy instead of strategy that is driven by timid budgets. "We have no more fussing around for months in the fall," says Chuck Bowman, director of planning and analysis at SPX. "There's no more messing around with huge planning documents and worrying about sandbagging and things like that. It is gone."

If this sounds too good to be true, listen to the comments of Thomas Clark, chief executive of Alltrista Corporation, the company that makes Ball home canning jars. Alltrista has been on an EVA bonus plan since 1992. "We have implemented EVA in such a way that we are out of the negotiating game," says Clark. "We used to spend the holiday season jockeying as to what the profit number ought to be for the year because the target hadn't been set for incentive compensation. But since 1992 I probably have seen 85 operating plans, and I've had to mandate a change in just one of them, and that was a relatively minor change."

A second and equally vivid change upon shifting to an EVA bonus system is an acute increase in capital consciousness on the part of managers. Balance sheet considerations become remarkably simple and automatic, because plan participants understand that EVA is calculated by imposing what amounts to a rental charge on capital and deducting it from net operating profits. All EVA companies have stories to tell about ways that EVA bonuses brought immediate improvements in capital productivity. Sun International in South Africa, for instance, is the owner of Sun City, an over-the-top oasis of gambling and fantasy in the former free state of Bophuthatswana. When Sun City went on EVA incentives, the manager of the lowest-priced hotel in the complex had been arguing to put safes, a regular feature in upscale South African hotels, in every room. He went ahead with the plan, but only after changing his specification from one of the most expensive to one of the cheapest safes on the market. After one retail chain adopted EVA, its store managers began putting new fixtures out for bid instead of routinely dealing with the same suppliers.

A fascinating academic study confirms this anecdotal evidence, and shows that EVA bonuses really do change management behavior in important ways. James Wallace, a professor of accounting at the University of California at Irvine, did his PhD dissertation on the effects of residual-income (that is, EVA) incentives on management actions. Wallace examined behavior by comparing companies that had recently adopted EVA bonus plans with peer companies in the same industries over the same years. He reasoned that firms adopting EVA bonus plans should be more willing to dispose of underperforming assets and more willing to return excess cash to shareholders. He also expected that these plans would bring a more efficient use of capital as measured by such things as turnover ratios for working capital and total assets.

Wallace found that the dollar amount of new investment did indeed decline while asset dispositions increased. Before adopting the new incentive plans, the companies were adding to capital faster than their peers; afterward, they were spending less capital. Stock repurchases increased, indicating that the companies were returning the funds from asset dispositions to shareholders rather than engaging in empire building. Before the change to EVA, share repurchases were higher at the peer companies. Asset turnover increased, and EVA itself shot up. Most important, the stocks of the EVA companies significantly outperformed those of their peers. Wallace also looked at the performance of companies that were using EVA to measure performance but were not using it as the basis of incentives. "This group exhibited much weaker or nonexistent results, which is what I had posited at the outset," says Wallace. "If the EVA measure is not taken to the level of compensation, it may not have any impact at all."

What every company wants is a culture of continuous improvement, responsibility, and accountability. Enlightened companies today also want all of their employees to feel involved, to be creative, and to welcome if not precipitate change. In other words, they want to instill an ownership culture that eliminates the need to constantly control behavior from above. To achieve that, what every company needs is an incentive system that clearly, objectively, predictably, and continuously rewards managers for creating shareholder wealth and penalizes them for destroying it. That's what EVA bonus plans do.

8

Banking on EVA

Each month the 500 salespeople at North Carolina's Centura Banks get personal tracking reports containing more information about their performances than most people ever see. The reports include the individual's sales of the bank's 56 product offerings, each of which has a specific "valued-added component" that is determined by deducting all the costs associated with it, including a charge for the cost of capital. The tracking report tots up the value added from product sales and then deducts the salesperson's salary, fringe benefits, travel costs, and entertainment expenses; the costs of support staff; a share of overhead expenses; and a few other adjustments. At the bottom is the personal EVA, 10% or 12% of which (depending on its size) the salesperson collects in a bonus paid out quarterly. A few salespeople have been able to double their total compensation since 1994, when Centura became the first U.S. bank to adopt EVA.

Since Centura, EVA has spread to more than a dozen other banks in the United States. ABSA, the largest bank in South Africa, implemented EVA in 1996, and ANZ Bank in Australia uses EVA incentives. Banc One, with assets in the $100 billion range, has the distinction of being the largest banking institution to adopt EVA. In 1995, CEO John McCoy decided to change the bank's structure from a federation of autonomous banks to a centralized national operation. McCoy wanted a standard performance measurement system that would focus all parts of the organization on long-term growth. At the suggestion of board member Fred Stratton, chairman of Briggs & Stratton, McCoy investigated EVA and then hired Stern Stewart to design a pilot program for strategic planning and both bank and nonbank operating units. Banc One began rolling out the EVA incentives and financial management system on a broader basis in 1997.

EVA came comparatively late to banks, partly because they used to be insulated from takeover threats and had little incentive to perform and compete except in size. In addition, the salad years of the nineties have had many bankers believing they are doing just fine with their existing management systems. In fact, conventional measures of profitability are just as dysfunctional in banking and other financial service companies as they are anywhere else. The GAAP calculations of bank earnings and balance sheets contain the same types of errors that distort the accounting statements of nonfinancial companies. As a result, strategies based on maximizing performance as measured by conventional accounting benchmarks can give the wrong signals. Ones based on maximizing growth in earnings can lead to rapid expansion in product areas that appear profitable only because their costs leave out any provision for the required return on equity capital. Strategies that focus on profitability and cost containment can blind managers to attractive growth opportunities. Heavily capitalized banks can be misled by seemingly favorable average returns on assets (ROA) and ratios of operating expenses to operating revenues (efficiency ratios) because neither contains a charge for the required returns on their hefty equity pools.

EVA, with its explicit recognition of the cost of equity capital, provides a far better gauge of bank performance. Statistical research by Stern Stewart and by Henry C. Dickson, head of bank analysis at

Salomon Brothers Smith Barney, shows that, just as in other industries, EVA correlates more highly with changes in banks' MVAs than any other performance measure. "We believe that EVA is a more effective predictive tool than other traditional bank stock valuation methods, and that it better highlights the more significant sources of value creation for the industry," Dickson wrote in a 1997 Smith Barney report titled "EVA & Bank Stock Valuation." EVA also provides a superior framework for dealing with some of the most difficult issues in banking, including capital allocation, relationship profitability, funds transfer pricing, and risk management. A number of special issues complicate the application of EVA to financial institutions, but the end result is just as effective as in other industries.

That certainly has been the case at Transamerica, the financial services giant, which adopted EVA back in 1991. Prior to EVA, Transamerica managed each of its business units to achieve high return-on-equity targets, though it paid bonuses on negotiated targets for net income. "If you go back to 1989, the companies with the lowest returns consumed all the capital, while the companies with the highest returns were just paying them out to the parent," says Thomas J. Cusack, who was in strategic planning and business development back then and now is CEO of Transamerica Life Company. The behavior Cusack describes is precisely what one should expect from ROE targets: Low-return businesses try to spend their way out of trouble, while high-return businesses are reluctant to invest for fear of lowering their average rate of return. Since going on EVA, however, Transamerica has been selling the low-return businesses, including a property and casualty insurer and a stake in a London insurance broker. "We use EVA in all our key decisions," says Cusack, "and we have had much better capital efficiency in all our businesses. After 15 years of unspectacular performance, we have outperformed the S&P ever since making the change to EVA."

As with all companies, the first steps in calculating a bank's EVA are the accounting adjustments necessary to eliminate distortions in net operating profits and capital. Under conventional accounting, banks have to write off a portion of each loan, in the form of a provision for prospective loan losses, as soon as they make it. Unsurprisingly, many bankers do not want to write loans in the last days of a quarter, or especially a year, because the full addition to the loan-loss reserve hits their earnings statements right away. Some have even been known to offer a lower rate if a borrower would wait until January to borrow the funds. What's more, the practice of charging earnings for *future* loan losses gives bankers little incentive to prevent their existing loans from going bad; the losses on those loans already have been charged against earnings. EVA eliminates both of those perverse incentives by substituting actual net charge-offs of bad loans for the loan-loss provision on the income statement to reflect current rather than anticipated losses. EVA also treats the accumulated reserve for loan losses as equity capital on which a return must be earned until loans actually are written off.

As with industrial and nonfinancial service companies, under EVA cash tax payments are substituted for the book tax provision. Restructuring charges are added back to net operating profits after taxes (NOPAT) and capital, treating them as resource redeployments that do not reduce total capital. Goodwill amortization is added back to NOPAT, and previously amortized goodwill is added to equity capital. These and other adjustments translate accounting earnings into an economic (or cash flow–based) NOPAT, and provide a more accurate—and higher—measure of the equity capital for which managers are responsible.

The cost of capital presents special issues for banks. They have to measure the relative risks of different business units and products and then allocate capital among them in order to get an accurate EVA measure for each. Stern Stewart has developed proprietary techniques that use the volatility of a business unit's NOPAT to assess relative risk and allocate capital. The approach has the advantage of being portable across varying lines of business, and allows banks to calculate the EVA of individual products and even customers.

Centura Banks, Inc., is one of the most innovative and respected small banks in the United States. Created in 1990 through a merger of two Rocky Mount, North Carolina, banks—People's and Planter's—Centura started life with assets of around $2 billion and increased that to $7 billion by 1997. It is the smallest bank that competes statewide in North Carolina, against foes like First Union and Nationsbank. Centura adopted EVA because then CEO Robert Mauldin felt he needed a more precise measure of performance than standard indicators such as earnings and return on equity. At the time, Centura was going through a transformation from a conventional small bank to a "retailer of financial services," including stocks, bonds, annuities, and insurance. Says Mauldin: "Management had to ask the question, 'What do we have to show for it? Are we creating value for our shareholders and how do we measure it?' "

Ever since, a rigorous adherence to EVA analysis has guided Centura to the most profitable paths. "EVA is a discipline that keeps you in the fairway," says Cecil Sewell, Jr., who succeeded Mauldin as CEO in 1997. "It's not the same fairway that would be dictated by earnings per share or generally accepted accounting principles, and it is interesting how it varies." EVA analysis infuses every aspect of the bank's work—from incentive systems to pricing of products, the tracking of sales results, the type and location of physical facilities, the purchase of new technology, and decisions on acquisitions, divestitures, and share repurchase plans. (See Figure 8.1.)

One major change is that Centura is no longer building new branches. It already had 154 and discovered that additional branches consume too much capital. (The only exceptions to the rule are acquisitions and the replacement of one or more branches with a new facility.) Instead of adding to its bricks and mortar, Centura has installed mini-branches in the Hannaford supermarket chain. The supermarket kiosklike branches are open seven days a week for a total of 60 hours and are staffed with salespeople who offer the full line of bank products. The staff is instructed to get out of their corrals and wander the aisles, meeting prospective customers. All branches are now officially called "financial centers."

Figure 8.1

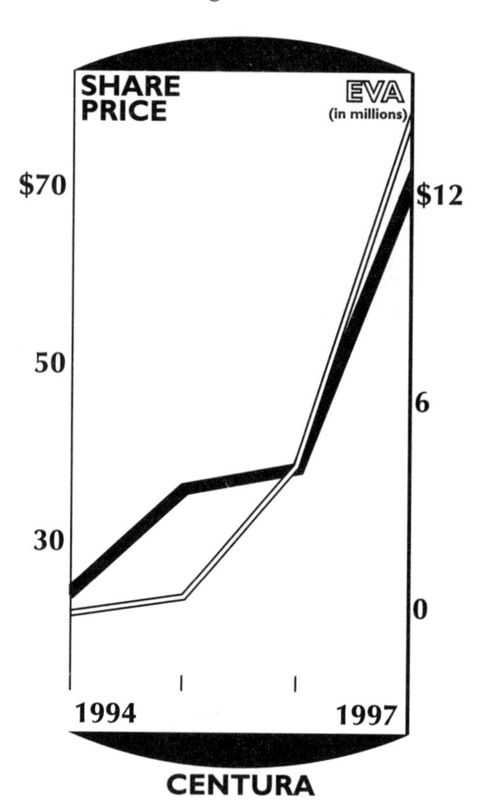

The term "loan officer" has also been discarded, and all salespeople are financial services officers, or FSOs.

Unsurprisingly, given the commission plan, EVA has made the sales staff acutely aware of the varying profitability of the products the bank offers. Loans and deposits, for example, are less profitable than non–balance sheet items like fees for letters of credit and commissions on the sales of securities, annuities, and insurance. Many salespeople were surprised to discover that deposits were often more profitable than loans. The reason: Centura has a comparatively large base of core deposits in checking and savings accounts, which cost substantially less than funds acquired in the money markets. Moreover, deposits often generate fee income from other products bought by the customer. The moral was not to curb the loan portfolio, but to build up the deposit base.

The EVA commission system met with some initial resistance and a lot of anxiety. Willard Ross, a group market manager who supervises eight regional markets with 120 salespeople, says that at first there was widespread shock: "They were afraid they wouldn't be able to sell enough and would be fired." Those fears quickly passed, however, and the new system revolutionized work habits. "Traditionally, bankers did not go out of the bank," says Vinton Fountain, a regional market manager. "Traditionally, the client contacted the banker. Bankers tended to be order takers." No longer. The FSOs have become more aggressive, buttonholing current customers to get new business and pursuing new prospects, preferably by referral. Willard Ross has set a goal for his people of 10 sales appointments a week. They now have time for this because their administrative duties have been shifted to service personnel. Also unsurprisingly, the new system has concentrated attention on the products that contribute the most EVA. Fountain maintains that his people have "profitability by product" fixed in their mind's eye. "In the old days," he says, "we spent 100% of our time pursuing loans and deposits. Now we spend 50% selling other products." Adds Ron Day, another regional market manager: "You may not work harder, but you work more effectively."

The sales staff has also been helped by the use of EVA on the account level, monitoring the profitability of individual accounts and customers. While there is no overall profile, the unprofitable customer tends to be someone who visits the bank a lot, consuming staff time, maintains several accounts with low balances, and doesn't buy any of the bank's ancillary products. The common banker's solution is to try to sell the chap a new product, but Centura's experience is that the new product is also likely to be unprofitable due to the customer's deplorable habits. The bank cannot get rid of its costly clients, but account analysis enables salespeople to concentrate on better prospects.

The EVA treatment of capitalizing rather than expensing R&D outlays reinforced Centura's predilection to spend heavily on alternative delivery systems in order to economize on the capital invested in serving its customers. It was the first bank in North Carolina to provide on-line banking, through Quicken or Microsoft Money. A much bigger investment has gone into the Centura Highway, a sophisticated system of telephone banking. Routine requests for information and other service calls are handled by a computerized voice response unit, with the customer reacting to recorded directions. A single transaction costs less than a penny, far less than an encounter with a human teller. Customers can also opt for a live voice at the end of the line and can arrange to take out a loan or buy an annuity, an insurance policy, or securities. Some three-quarters of all sales that result from Centura's direct-mail promotions are consummated over the telephone. The savings in costs, with an attendant boost to EVA, are enormous as use of the Highway increases.

EVA has been the key consideration in potential acquisitions, which have been part of everyday life at Centura since its inception. Many candidates seemed enticing when viewed in terms of the contribution to earnings but became decidedly less attractive when the cost of capital entered the equation. Over the past few years, Centura rejected a dozen or more prospects that looked desirable on an earnings basis but failed to clear the EVA hurdle. In two cases, EVA analysis pared down the price that Centura paid for acquisitions. It bought the Cleveland Federal Savings and Loan in Shelby, North Carolina, for $16.4 million and the First Southern Savings and Loan in Asheboro, North Carolina, for $59.4 million. In both cases, Centura offered less than it would otherwise have bid if not for EVA. In another case a couple of years ago, Centura reluctantly walked away from a candidate because the asking price was too high. Mauldin and Sewell watched regretfully as a rival bought the bank—regretfully, that is, until the buyer's stock price declined.

The drive to maximize EVA is motivated by more than intellectual persuasion, since EVA growth is the key ingredient in the incentive bonus plan that covers senior executives. Centura exceeded its EVA improvement targets—and managers have collected correspondingly high bonuses—each year since going on EVA. In addition, some members of top management use a portion of their cash bonuses to buy leveraged stock options with exercise prices that escalate at a rate of about 6.5% a year. If shareholders do not get at least a 6.5% rate of return, the options are worthless. But the returns on the options skyrocket as the rate of price appreciation goes above 6.5%, as it has been doing since 1994.

EVA also has brought a new discipline to Centura. The bank used to be able to juggle accounting numbers so that it could "make earnings per share be anything we wanted it to be," says Sewell. "But you can't manage EVA. It's a much stricter analysis." The discipline has paid off. As Centura's EVA moved from minus $100,000 in 1994 to $4.2 million in 1996, the stock price jumped from $24.375 to $44.625, and by the spring of 1998 the shares were trading above $70.

9

The EVA Financial Management System

EVA performs so well as the framework for a comprehensive financial management system because the EVA measure itself packs enormous analytical power, revealing far more about the underlying dynamics of a business than any other managerial tool. Yet EVA also is surprisingly easy to communicate to nonfinancial managers and even to rank-and-file workers, providing everyone in an organization with the same clear objective—to increase EVA as much as possible. When EVA becomes the singular focus for all decisions, it establishes clear and accountable links between strategic thinking, capital investments, daily operating decisions, and shareholder value. In the process, it can foster an uncommon sense of partnership and cooperation among corporate functions and operating divisions that are at sixes and sevens in many organizations.

The most obvious way that EVA helps managers make better decisions is by charging their operations for the cost of all capital. The capital charge compels managers to use assets more diligently by focusing them directly on the costs associated with such things as inventories, receivables, and capital equipment. Viewed another way, the capital charge effectively converts the balance sheet into another line-item expense that managers can compare with, and weigh against, all other costs. It enables managers to routinely and automatically consider the cost of capital in every decision, and to accurately assess the trade-offs between operating costs and capital costs.

Some trade-offs are simple. Is it a good idea to buy materials in larger batches at lower prices? That reduces unit costs but increases inventory days on hand. Other trade-offs are more managerial in scope, and some are downright strategic. Does it make sense to charge a lower price or to provide more service? Would it pay to have a higher market share or a higher profit margin? How much is too much to pay for an acquisition? Such questions can be tough to answer when a particular choice would, for example, cause earnings to rise and return on assets to fall. But the right answer is clear for the EVA company: whatever will produce the highest EVA over time. Says George Harad, CEO of Boise Cascade, which went on EVA in 1995: "When you make the cost of capital a dollar measure down through the organization, people pay closer attention to the investment on hand. We have been pleased and surprised. Most of our managers are financially sophisticated, but it has made a significant difference."

Charging for capital is only the beginning. EVA also eliminates distortions that plague conventional accounting. As mentioned earlier, generally accepted accounting principles are ridden with anomalies that misrepresent the true economics of a business. Standard accounting, for example, penalizes managers for increased spending on innovation and brand building. It makes it hard for them to jettison poorly performing assets and restructure. It causes aggressive financing to make poor investments look like winners, and distorts true performance in many other ways as well. By making just a handful of changes to GAAP, including such things as capitalizing research and development outlays and eliminating goodwill write-offs, EVA removes the most destructive of these distortions so that managers can make better assessments of the impact that their actions have on true economic profits. (See Chapter 11 for a discussion of how to calculate EVA.)

Eliminating the distortions in conventional accounting and charging for the cost of capital make EVA a measure of far greater significance than most people realize. By accounting correctly for the economics of the business and by subtracting the cost of all resources required to produce revenues, including the cost of capital, EVA accurately captures the combined productivity of all factors of production in a single measure. As Peter Drucker put it in a 1995 *Harvard Business Review* article: "By measuring the value added over *all* costs, including the cost of capital, EVA measures, in effect, the productivity of all factors of production. It does not, by itself, tell us why a certain product or a certain service does not add value or what to do about it. But it shows us what we need to find out and whether we need to take remedial action. EVA should also be used to find out what works. It does show which product, service, operation or activity has unusually high productivity and adds unusually high value. Then we should ask ourselves, What can we learn from those successes?"

Combining operating costs and capital costs in a single profit measure that is expressed in dollars rather than a rate of return gives EVA another unique quality. It means that more EVA always is better than less—that a larger economic profit always is better than a smaller one. That cannot be said of any other performance measure. Continuously increasing sales, margins, earnings, or return on investment, or any of the measures typically appearing on a "balanced scorecard," is not necessarily good. Each can be pursued to the point that further "improvement" actually erodes economic performance and shareholder wealth. Higher earnings, for example, are thought to be unequivocally good, but you cannot tell whether more earnings really are better unless you know how much additional capital was needed to produce the increase. In other words, *EVA is the only reliable and unambiguous continuous-improvement metric*. In fact, a big part of the case for EVA is the case against all other financial measures; all of them, as you will see, can mislead and cause managers to make wrong decisions.

The final ingredient in the power of EVA is the ease with which employees at all levels can grasp it and put it to use. Says Rodney Carter, director of the EVA implementation project at J.C. Penney, in explaining why the giant retailer decided to adopt EVA in 1996: "We wanted to have something that operating management can understand and use—that provides a common language that is understandable and actionable." One reason that Herman Miller adopted EVA was to increase business literacy among its workers. Says CFO Brian Walker: "We've gotten a buy-in all the way down to the shop floor to a greater degree than anyone thought we ever could, and we have increased the business literacy of those people in a way that they understand analytical tools and techniques that they never knew before."

To illustrate his point, Walker tells the story of an outside director who was extremely skeptical that rank-and-file workers would understand the new system and worried that it was too complex a measure to use in the company's gain-sharing programs. About six months after implementing EVA, Herman Miller held a board meeting at a seating factory. During a tour of the plant, the skeptical director walked up to a sewing-machine operator and asked her to explain EVA. "And this lady began to explain what EVA is," says Walker. "She said, 'Well, you look at both expense and your assets and it helps you decide how you better allocate your resources between the two and what the most effective way is. It lets you realize that even the assets have a cost.'

"The director was pretty intrigued that she knew the answer, so then he asked her, 'Well, how does it change your work?' And she said, 'Well, the difference today is that we used to have these stacks of fabric sitting here on the tables waiting until we needed them. And we didn't understand that that actually cost money to us. We were going to use the fabric anyway, so who cares that we're buying it and stacking it up here? Now no one has excess fabric. They only have the stuff that they're actually working on today. And it's changed the way we think about how we connect with suppliers, and we're having the suppliers deliver fabric more often.' This is a lady who simply runs a sewing machine." The director asked the same questions of other workers as he walked through the plant, and kept getting similar responses. Finally, he turned to Walker and said, "Okay, I give. You guys have been able to do it. I don't know how you did it, but you were able to do it."

The main reason EVA is so easy to communicate is that it starts with the familiar concept of operating profits and simply adds one more expense, which is the charge for the cost of capital. The capital charge is easily explained as a sort of rental charge on the capital used by a company, division, or business unit. The dynamics of the capital charge and EVA are equally simple. A reduction in the amount of capital needed to produce a given product or service brings a lower capital charge and higher EVA, while any new investment will boost EVA only if it produces a large enough increase in operating profits to cover the added capital charge.

Operating profits is a term that needs explanation here because it has so many variations nowadays. The version of operating profits used in EVA is net operating profits after taxes, or NOPAT for short. Unlike the operating profits calculated by many companies, NOPAT includes deductions for taxes and for depreciation of equipment. Both are subtracted from NOPAT because they are genuine costs that have to be managed. Moving from NOPAT to EVA is merely a matter of subtracting the capital charge, which is calculated by multiplying the net working capital and fixed assets used in an operation by the percentage cost of capital. The remainder—the residual—is the dollar amount by which profits exceed or fall short of all costs, including the minimum rate of return on capital. Arithmetically, the formula looks like this:

$$
\begin{array}{rl}
 & \text{Sales} \\
- & \text{Operating costs} \\
- & \text{Capital costs} \\
\hline
= & \text{EVA}
\end{array}
$$

What does it mean if EVA is negative? Most people would answer that earnings are not sufficient to cover the cost of capital. That is a natural way to think about the issue since the cost of capital is what has been missing from conventional accounting. Suddenly including the cost of capital makes it appear that capital costs are what are making EVA negative. The fact that the providers of capital, or at least the providers of equity capital, get paid last also makes it natural to assume that their payments are making EVA negative. But what a negative EVA really means is that a company is not covering its costs, period. The order of subtraction does not matter. It is just as correct to say that a company isn't covering its labor costs, or distribution costs, or materials costs, or marketing costs as it is to say that a company is not covering its capital costs.

Saying that a company with negative EVA is not covering its capital costs is convenient shorthand for saying that it is losing money even though it may be reporting positive earnings. But this has the unfortunate side effect of conveying the impression that the cost of capital is somehow discretionary or special or different from other costs. It's not. It is just as inescapable as any other cost of doing business. The fact that standard accounting largely ignores the cost of capital does not make it any less real. To borrow from Robert Frost's criticism of free verse, one should as soon compute earnings without a capital charge "as play tennis with the net down." EVA simply lifts the net back up where it belongs. What a negative EVA does not mean is that a business unit automatically is a hopeless loser that should be shuttered or sold. Because EVA is a continuous improvement metric, making a negative EVA less negative is just as wealth-creating as making a positive EVA more positive.

Companies reap the full benefits of EVA only when they use it as the centerpiece of their financial management system and as the deciding factor in all business decisions. Every company has a financial management system, though most, as we said in Chapter 1, are so complicated and confused that they hardly justify use of the word "system." The confusion arises from the fact that most companies employ a numbing array of measures to express financial goals and objectives. Strategic plans may be based on growth in earnings or revenues or market share (though rarely on shareholder wealth itself). Business units may be evaluated by return on investment or against a budgeted profit level. Individual products or product lines typically are judged by gross margins, cash flow, or market share. Finance departments usually analyze capital investments in terms of discounted cash flow and net present value, but weigh prospective acquisitions by the likely contribution to growth in earnings or earnings per share. What's more, all those measures (other than net present value) are poorly correlated with shareholder wealth, and often are contradictory or conflicting in the sense that an increase in one will sometimes bring a decrease in another.

The result of using inconsistent standards, goals, and terminology usually is incohesive planning, operating strategy, and decision making. With conflicting messages from different measures, the stage is set to perpetuate battles between warring staff fiefdoms, to politicize measures in the sense that managers will pick and choose until they find one that supports what they want to do, and to promote dysfunctional, wealth-destroying behavior. Negotiated profit plans, which are a part of most conventional financial management systems, foster "satisficing" rather than maximizing behavior. Managers under conventional systems also tend to be preoccupied with profit margins and are reluctant to price aggressively in the pursuit of growth, or to cannibalize current business with new technology even when it is clear that the technology is essential to the long-run welfare of the company. Throw in a few mandates from corporate about quality and customer satisfaction, and line managers often have no idea where their true priorities should lie.

The EVA financial management system eliminates conflict and confusion by couching all business issues—starting with strategy and moving all the way down to daily operating decisions—in the context of the impact on EVA. This allows all financial decisions to be modeled, monitored, evaluated, communicated, and compensated in terms of a single measure, and provides a common language for employees across all operating and staff functions. Using one measure as the basis for all decisions—something that no other management system provides—is what unites all employees in the pursuit of the single goal of creating value. Other measures remain, of course. Managers still have to worry about margins, turnover ratios, unit costs, cycle times, and a host of other variables, but the worrying is always in the context of their impact on EVA. The focus on a single measure also simplifies decisions enormously. Communication channels are strengthened, decision making speeds up, teamwork rises, and parochial behavior declines when everyone is pulling on the same oar.

The mandate under an EVA management system, as we have said, is to increase EVA as much as possible in order to maximize shareholder wealth. The arithmetic of EVA shows that companies have only four ways of doing that:

1. Cut costs, and reduce taxes, to boost NOPAT without adding to capital. That is, operate more efficiently to earn a higher return on the capital already invested in the business.
2. Undertake all investments in which the increase in NOPAT will be greater than the increase in the capital charge. That is, invest in *profitable* growth by undertaking all positive net-present-value projects that promise to produce a return on capital that exceeds the cost of the capital.
3. Pull capital out of operations when the savings from the reduction in the capital charge exceeds any reduction in NOPAT. That is, stop investing in—or liquidate—assets and activities that are not generating returns equal to or greater

than the cost of capital. The big changes in this area are selling assets that are worth more to others, but the category also includes such things as reducing inventories and speeding up collection of accounts receivable (both of which represent investments of capital).

4. Structure the finances of the company in a way that minimizes the cost of capital, something that is purely within the demesne of the finance department, the CEO, and the board of directors.

Financial strategy can have a significant effect on the cost of capital and thus on EVA and market value. The basic building blocks of financial strategy are the mix of debt and equity on a company's balance sheet and the method—dividends or share repurchases—that it uses to distribute cash to shareholders. (The type of debt—fixed-rate or floating, straight or convertible—and matters such as the voting rights of various classes of stock also affect the cost of capital.) The seminal work of Nobel laureates Franco Modigliani and Merton Miller in the late 1950s established that the deductibility of interest payments makes debt a cheaper source of financing than equity for companies with taxable profits. Superficially, this would imply that companies should be financed almost entirely with debt and just a sliver of equity, but that is a dangerous oversimplification.

In fact, the optimal use of debt must take into consideration the inherent riskiness of a company's business and the funding requirements of its operating strategy. Companies with comparatively low risk and stable cash flows can afford a high ratio of debt to equity, while high-risk companies need to keep debt low enough to ensure that their cash flows will cover interest costs in bad times. That's why electric utilities historically have been highly leveraged (though deregulation has increased their risks and reduced their ability to carry leverage in recent years), while start-up companies are financed almost entirely with equity. Similarly, growth companies and companies with hearty appetites for acquisitions need more financing flexibility, in the form of unused debt capacity, than nonacquisitive companies in mature industries, though many companies operate with costly excess debt capacity to finance potential acquisitions that never seem to happen. What all this means is that the optimal financial structure for any company to minimize the cost of capital is the highest proportion of debt that is consistent with the riskiness of its business and the financing flexibility that its investment and acquisition strategies demand.

The choice of dividends or share repurchases to distribute excess cash to shareholders also affects the optimal debt/equity mix. That is because boards of directors are loath to cut dividends, which makes them a sort of fixed charge against cash flows from operations. Thus, dividends reduce borrowing capacity by reducing the amount of cash available to service debt, and also limit management's ability to use cash flows from operations to finance investments or acquisitions. Companies have far more flexibility, and can carry more debt on their balance sheets, when they use share repurchases instead of dividends to distribute cash. Share repurchases also have the advantage of being a more tax-efficient way to distribute cash. Taxable shareholders pay taxes at ordinary income rates on the full amount of their dividend receipts, but they pay taxes at lower capital gains rates on share repurchases, and then only the portion of the proceeds that constitutes a taxable gain.

The foregoing is what might be called static financial policy. Finance can have a dynamic dimension as well. The leveraged buyout movement of the eighties demonstrated that high levels of debt can have a highly salutary effect on management behavior, especially for companies that do not need significant financing flexibility. When a company is operating close to the edge in terms of its ability to generate sufficient cash flows to cover its debt obligations, it has the effect of focusing managers much more intently on maximizing performance, wiping out the complacency that too often comes with a comfy cushion of free cash flow. One dynamic approach to financial policy is to issue a large amount of debt and repurchase shares. That puts managers in an LBO-like situation as they scramble to meet the interest obligations and pay down debt. Then, once the debt is substantially paid off the company does the same thing all over again.

What such a company is doing, in effect, is repeatedly borrowing large amounts of money to prepay what otherwise would be five or 10 years' worth of dividends or share repurchases by means of a large share repurchase now, and using cash flows from subsequent operations to repay the "dividend loan." The extremely high leverage that this approach entails also has the effect of minimizing what Harvard professor Michael Jensen and others have taken to calling "reinvestment risk," or the risk that managers in mature industries will waste excess cash flow by overinvesting in their core businesses or needlessly diversifying.

Finding the optimal financial strategy can reinforce the changes in operating strategy that EVA brings to a company and increase shareholder wealth by reducing the cost of capital. In 1997, for example, Stern Stewart developed financial strategies for three companies that boosted their combined market values by almost $500 million. The first, in February, involved IPALCO, the parent of Indianapolis Power and Light, and was the first leveraged recapitalization ever by an electric utility. IPALCO used a five-year bank loan to repurchase more than 12.5 million shares of its common stock, or more than 21% of the shares outstanding, at a total cost of some $400 million. The company also cut its annual cash dividend from $1.48 to $1 a share, and reduced its target payout ratio (dividends as a percentage of earnings) from the traditional utility norm of more than 70% to a range of 45% to 50%.

The repurchase, which was done at a premium to the market value through a Dutch-auction form of tender offer, gave income-oriented investors a chance to exit the stock on favorable terms, while the change in financial structure and lower payout ratio gave IPALCO greater financial flexibility going forward as it moves into an increasingly competitive environment. (In a Dutch auction, the company sets a price range at which it will buy shares and allows shareholders to tender shares at prices within that range; the company then pays the lowest price that will get the number of shares it wants.) IPALCO's stock jumped 12.4% when it announced the recap and beat the Standard & Poor's electric utility index by 20 percentage points in the weeks following the announcement.

Two months later, Briggs & Stratton and SPX Corporation also announced Dutch-auction share repurchases. Briggs repurchased 3.6 million of its 29 million shares outstanding, a move that sent its stock up 12.3% on the day of the announcement. SPX's was the most radical restructuring of the three. Several months before, SPX had completed the sale of its piston-ring business to Dana Corporation, and used the proceeds to buy in $128 million of subordinated notes that carried onerously restrictive covenants. That freed it up to negotiate a $400-million bank credit agreement and make a tender offer for 2.7 million, or 18%, of its shares outstanding. SPX also eliminated its dividend. SPX stock, which already had risen from less than $15 a share to $45.625 since the company adopted EVA the year before, shot up another 14%, to $52.50, on news of the buyback.

Most followers of SPX, who knew that CEO John Blystone planned to grow the company by acquisition, had expected him to sit on the cash from the sale to Dana until he found something to buy. But with no attractive candidates immediately available, Blystone figured it was better to return cash to shareholders once he had freed himself of the restrictions imposed by the subordinated notes. Eliminating the dividend enhanced the company's financing flexibility, and Blystone reasoned that the company's obvious commitment to shareholder value would give SPX ample access to new funds when he did find an attractive acquisition. Meanwhile, the higher debt ratio reduced SPX's cost of capital and boosted EVA.

As mentioned earlier, Briggs & Stratton refers to the first three types of EVA improvement—the ones available to operating managers—as operate, build, and harvest, terms that nicely capture the dynamics of the changes involved and make it easier to explain them to line managers and rank-and-file workers. SPX refers to them, respectively, as continuous improvement, growth, and rightsizing. But however they are titled, few things in the real world fall neatly into just one of the three categories. Consolidating facilities in a restructuring, for example, obviously involves harvesting the assets that are sold, but it usually requires what properly should be thought of as an investment in severance pay to reduce ongoing operating expenses. Most of the major operating improvements that fall under the rubric of reengineering entail using a small amount of additional capital in order to eliminate a large amount of unnecessary labor, or a small amount of added labor in order to get large increases in the productivity of capital equipment.

Indeed, it is difficult to think of any meaningful change in the way that a company does business that doesn't affect both operating costs on the income statement and capital costs on the balance sheet—which is precisely why EVA is such an effective tool for operating managers, and why every other measure can mislead. When managers are evaluated purely on the basis of operating profits, they naturally treat capital as though it were free, and wind up using far too much of it. But when their performance is measured in terms of EVA, managers automatically take the balance-sheet impact of their decisions into account.

An experience at the Quaker Oats Company provides a telling case in point. Before Quaker Oats adopted EVA in 1992, Steve Brunner, the manager of Quaker's granola bar plant in Danville, Illinois, used long production runs to turn out the various sizes of bars in order to minimize downtime and setup costs. The long runs bolstered operating profits and minimized unit costs, but they also resulted in huge inventories of bars that sat in a warehouse until they gradually were shipped to customers. When the EVA capital charge was added to Brunner's performance measure, he immediately switched to short production runs in order to eliminate most of the inventory. NOPAT and the profit margin declined (and unit production costs rose) because of the more frequent setups, but the capital charge declined even more, so EVA increased. Before EVA, says Brunner, "I had never considered spending a dollar to reduce my use of capital." Smaller inventories were only part of the benefit, by the way. Because the granola bars moved out of the plant faster than before, they arrived fresher in stores, and customer satisfaction rose. Quaker Oats is something less than an unbridled success story, of course, because it grossly overpaid in its acquisition of Snapple Beverage Corporation. Top management bypassed the EVA analysis of the acquisition because it was determined to pick up the brand at any cost for "strategic" reasons. Today, Snapple is gone, the CEO is gone, but EVA remains and the stock price is well on the road to a dramatic recovery.

The Coca-Cola Company discovered a similar trade-off between operating and capital costs when it adopted EVA in the mid-1980s. Coke had been shipping its soft-drink syrup to bottlers in stainless steel cans, which lasted for years and could be reused over and over. Once it went on EVA, however, Coke switched to cardboard containers that it uses once and throws away. The change reduced both operating profits and profit margins because it boosted total operating costs and unit costs. Those are bad things, of course, but in this case and the Quaker Oats example, the savings in capital costs outweighed the hit to the income statement.

As the Quaker Oats and Coke examples show, maximizing operating profits or profit margins is not necessarily the way to maximize economic profits and shareholder wealth, because operating profits ignore capital costs. And as Coca-Cola learned with stainless steel cans, the capital asset does not have to be major; everything that ties up money matters. In an employee brochure titled *Accountability for EVA*, Coke notes that "Something as simple as just relocating some of our vending machines increased our EVA." Moving the machines did so, obviously, by increasing the sales per machine, but what a change like that actually represents is a more effective deployment of capital equipment.

Other conventional measures of performance are equally flawed or even more so. To see what we mean, look at the performance of Wal-Mart in its great growth decades of the seventies and eighties. In nearly all of those years, Wal-Mart had negative cash flows from operations net of new investment spending, or what is known as free cash flow. Sam Walton was opening new stores so fast that he couldn't finance them with cash from current operations, and constantly was raising new money to fund his expansion. As it turned out, the returns on the new stores averaged around 25%, which was much higher than Wal-Mart's cost of capital of around 12.5%, making Sam's negative free cash flows a great thing because they fueled phenomenal growth in the company's EVA. Indeed, they were one of the greatest things a manager ever did for shareholders. Wal-Mart's return to investors over that period was among the best in the world, and Sam became the richest man in America. The point is that free cash flow, while a valid measure of the company's value when projected into the future, is useless as an indication of current performance.

Wal-Mart's history also vividly demonstrates how something as clear and simple as profit margin can mislead. Wal-Mart's EVA soared from $30 million in 1980 to $528 million in 1990, and the stock market reacted by lifting its MVA from $664 million to $28.3 billion. Kmart, in contrast, turned in a doggy performance over the decade. Its EVA fell from minus $43 million to minus $172 million, bringing a drop in MVA from minus $505 million to minus $1.3 billion, and this in a period when the vast majority of companies enjoyed large increases in their MVAs. Most people would assume that Wal-Mart must have had higher profit margins than Kmart. In fact, Kmart's gross margins averaged around 28% in those years (that is, the cost of goods sold was about 72% of sales), while Wal-Mart's gross margins often were as low as 23%.

So why was Wal-Mart a winner and Kmart a loser? Because Wal-Mart was using its *capital* more efficiently. In retailing, capital consists largely of store space and inventories. By giving up gross margin in order to draw customers into its stores with lower prices, Wal-Mart achieved much higher sales per square foot of floor space than Kmart or other discount retailers. And Wal-Mart's vaunted innovations in inventory control, including computerized systemwide tracking of goods on hand and automated reordering, enabled it to operate with the lowest inventories in the business. Wal-Mart, in other words, was the EVA—and stock market—winner because it employed much less capital per dollar of sales. Margins do matter, but only in the context of everything else; by themselves, they say next to nothing about performance.

What about return on assets (ROA) and its first cousin, return on net assets (RONA), as gauges of performance? Both are a major improvement over operating profits or earnings because they encourage a focus on the efficient management of assets. But any rate of return measure presents a number of practical and conceptual disadvantages, especially when it is used as the basis for incentive awards. Rates of return can be inflated by the use of operating leases and other off-balance-sheet financing. They can make past investments—what economists call sunk costs—appear relevant to decisions about future actions when they should not be. Moreover, rates of return that are calculated from conventional accounting statements share the same anomalies and distortions as accounting earnings.

Most important, maximizing rate of return and maximizing shareholder wealth are not the same thing. Remember that the principle directive of modern financial theory is that companies should undertake all investments with a positive NPV, which means all investments on which the expected rate of return exceeds the cost of capital. But if a company is trying to maximize ROA or RONA and its rate of return already is much higher than its cost of capital, it will reject any investment with an expected rate of return that is lower than the current rate, even if it is higher than the cost of capital. In other words, it will pass up many opportunities to create shareholder wealth. Alternatively, if the current rate of return is less than the cost of capital, the company or business unit can improve its rate of return by undertaking any new investment with a return greater than the current rate, even if it is lower than the cost of capital. Those two scenarios may sound extreme, but they accurately describe what usually happens when companies compensate managers on the basis of ROA or RONA. Those running the winning divisions turn down almost every investment proposal, and those in charge of the losing divisions are eager to invest in just about anything in order to spend their way out of their problems. Companies wind up feeding their dogs and starving their stars.

Applying EVA to capital budgeting involves only a modest revision in the mechanics of assessing prospective projects, but it brings about a radical change in the way projects are evaluated and in the behavior of managers. As we have said, most companies today use discounted cash flow analysis to screen capital spending projects. This involves estimating the cash flows that a project will generate each year, discounting them back to the present at an interest rate equal to the cost of capital, and subtracting the cost of the project to obtain its net present value, or NPV. The discounted cash flow approach is fine in principle, but has largely been a failure in practice.

The problem with using discounted cash flow to estimate NPV is that once a project has been approved and the money spent, hardly anyone ever checks to see if the actual cash flows lived up to projections. Instead, the investment is treated in ongoing performance assessments as if capital was free, with the business unit judged only on the operating profits it generates. Knowing this, division managers have an enormous incentive to bake the numbers in spending proposals, tweaking cash flow projections until they discount back to the present at a positive NPV. The corporate office knows perfectly well what is going on, of course, so it dispatches storm troopers from the controller's office to ask bothersome questions and challenge cash-flow forecasts. The divisions counter these moves by ginning their numbers still higher. In the end, the entire process is rife with mutual deception and Kabuki theater. Everyone is wearing a mask.

The EVA approach is mathematically identical to discounted cash flow, but the decision dynamics it gives rise to are radically different. Under EVA, the procedure for evaluating a project is to forecast the EVA it will generate each year and discount that back to the present. Since EVA already includes a charge for capital and for depreciation, there is no need to subtract the initial investment from the discounted future EVAs. The result is exactly the same—to the penny—as the NPV one gets by using discounted cash flow, but the process has several advantages. First, discounting EVA instead of cash flows enables division managers to use the same, consistent analytical framework in capital budgeting, annual profit planning, and day-to-day operations. Second, it allows managers to readily see the benefits from a capital project in terms of the EVA performance of their business unit. Third, it gives a more accurate portrayal of the yearly value added from a project; instead of recognizing the full cost of the investment up front—and then forgetting about it—EVA spreads the capital cost over the life of the project.

Most important, when managers are in an EVA bonus plan like the one described in Chapter 7, the EVA approach enforces capital discipline throughout the life of an investment. This, in effect, is NPV with a memory. Managers know that their future bonuses will suffer if a project fails to deliver positive EVA, so they no longer have an incentive to cook their forecasts. Instead, they have a powerful motivation to make the most accurate projections they can, and they spend money more carefully, more sparingly, and more intelligently. The corporate office, in turn, no longer needs to worry about the integrity of the capital spending proposals it gets from the field, and the need for storm troopers disappears. Instead of seeing the finance department as a niggardly Dr. No, operating divisions seek its help in sharpening their EVA forecasts.

The difference between the EVA approach and the conventional approach to capital budgeting reflects two diametrically opposed views of the world. While the conventional approach includes a nominal hurdle rate to get projects approved, the fact that it treats capital as if it was free once it is in place means that the demand for capital is virtually unlimited. As a result, top management has to set a limit on overall capital spending and then ration out the dollars to the managers who can tell the best story. Under EVA, in contrast, the corporate office acts like a bank. It makes capital readily available to the operating divisions, but only at a price, and the price automatically limits demand to the projects that managers genuinely believe will enhance shareholder wealth. If this sounds too good to be true, listen to Francis Corby, the CFO of Harnischfeger Industries, a manufacturer of capital equipment for the mining and paper industries that went on EVA in 1993: "We have not had a single capital budgeting project turned down since adopting EVA. If our operating managers have spent all this time convincing themselves that a project will return the cost of capital, and they are willing to risk their own capital on it in the form of their future bonuses, we give them the money. Our managers are spending money like it's their own, and that's paying dividends for us in many ways."

As explained in Chapter 3, a company's MVA is the stock market's assessment of the NPV of the company taken as a whole. Since the discounted present value of future EVA is mathematically identical to NPV, the present value of future EVA also is the same thing as the estimated contribution that a project will make to the firm's MVA. Thus, EVA enables managers to do much more than determine whether a project is sufficiently profitable. They can take their forecast of the future EVA of a project—or of a plant, a product line, a customer relationship, or anything else—and tie it back directly to its contribution to the value of the firm.

This makes EVA a wonderfully powerful tool for strategic planning and decision making. Managers, for example, can value an acquisition candidate in terms of the contribution to EVA, since an acquisition really is nothing more than another type of capital investment project. Top management can test whether the EVA from the sum of its business plans is consistent with the market value of the company. It can directly assess, based on the best estimates of its business unit managers, how much a strategic expansion into a new market or product area will add to or subtract from shareholder wealth. It can apply an analytical technique called EVA drivers, which disaggregates EVA into the contributions of a concise group of key operating variables, to benchmark performance and find out what's working and what isn't working. Managers can use EVA as a way to directly compare alternative strategies and identify the variables that shape the payoffs and find ways to improve them. They can use EVA goals as a way to set stretch targets, and then use the EVA drivers analysis to evaluate plans for achieving those goals.

10

Breaking the Regulatory Mould

Increasingly, EVA is attracting the attention and enthusiasm of top managers who are caught up in the global trend of privatizing state-owned businesses and the parallel move to greater freedom and competition in regulated industries. These companies are using EVA to accelerate the difficult but essential cultural transition from the comfortable, complacent world of monopoly to a competitive market environment. Even some agencies that may never be privatized, including an assortment of state-owned enterprises in New Zealand, are using EVA to promote operating efficiency and provide an objective basis for capital investment and pricing decisions. And the United States Postal Service, as you will see, is using EVA to achieve remarkable cost savings and service improvements that totally belie the image of a bloated, bumbling bureaucracy.

EVA is proving particularly popular among capital-intensive telecommunications companies. Following the lead of Sprint and AT&T in the United States, the Australian telecommunications company Telstra began implementing EVA in 1997 on the eve of the government's sale of its shares to the public. Embratel, the long-distance carrier in Brazil, and Telerj, which provides local telephone service in Rio de Janeiro, adopted EVA in anticipation of the privatization of their parent company, Telebras. And Telecom New Zealand, which was privatized in 1990 and faces competition as intense as any in the world, began using EVA informally in 1993 and did a full implementation, complete with uncapped bonuses and a bonus bank, in 1994.

In the United States, the unraveling of local power monopolies that the federal Department of Energy put in motion in the eighties has accelerated in the nineties as states have begun to adopt laws mandating open markets in electrical power generation and the sale of natural gas to end users. Local utilities retain their monopolies over the distribution of power, but in many cases are now delivering electricity or gas that is sold directly to the end user by a third party. Facing price competition for the first time can be a rather uncongenial experience for managers whose operating principle always has been to add as many assets as possible to the "rate base" (the assets and operating costs that regulators use in determining what price schedule will yield a "fair" return on investment), secure in the knowledge that state regulators would set prices high enough to recapture costs. In response, more than a half-dozen electric and gas utilities have seized on EVA as the quickest and most effective way to educate their managers in the ways of the competitive world, and to provide a consistent basis for managing—and comparing the performance of—their regulated and nonregulated businesses.

The Montana Power Company adopted EVA in 1997. Though small for a public utility, with revenues of just over $1 billion, Montana Power is one of the most innovative and broadly diversified energy companies in the United States. In addition to providing electricity to 282,000 customers in Montana, the company is in oil and gas production and coal mining. It sells a gamut of fuels from natural gas to oil, propane, and coal, and actively trades electricity and natural gas in the unregulated wholesale markets. Overseas, it has interests in an electric cogeneration facility in England, an independent power plant in Jamaica, and electric generating plants under development in India and Pakistan. And it has a telephone company. The Montana Power Telephone Company provides long-distance service and Internet connections locally and has a 3,000-mile fiber-optic network that wends from Minneapolis to Seattle. A second, 1,600-mile line, running from Portland, Oregon, to Los Angeles via Boise, Salt Lake City, and Las Vegas, will be operational in the second half of 1999.

Montana Power's implementation of EVA coincided with the passage of a state law mandating a four-year transition to open competition in electricity and natural gas sales. "Moving into deregulation, we knew our old measures weren't going to work," says B. Northey Tretheway, manager of financial services and leader of the EVA implementation team. "We wanted to stay out in front of other utilities in making the right decisions for shareholders." Shareholders certainly enjoyed the company's performance in 1997. The total return on its common stock was 58%, outperforming 90 of the 100 utilities tracked by the Edison Electric Institute, the industry trade group.

Only half jokingly, Tretheway says the most visible change brought by EVA has been unaccustomed anxiety on the part of many of the company's managers now that Montana Power is the first public utility to have adopted a full EVA incentive compensation system. The managers of the company's eight operating units and their direct reports get bonuses based primarily on the EVA performance of their individual businesses. "We have accountability where there wasn't any before," he says. "There was no need for efficiency or worrying about capital." Now, says Tretheway, managers in many of the business units have begun "a thought process on capital that wasn't there before." They have begun eyeing idle equipment for possible sale, and are rethinking when and how to enter into coal production leases that until now have provided a return of capital but no return on capital. In electrical generating, maintenance operations have become much more efficient because managers are considering, for the first time, how the timing of specific types of maintenance affects the energy needs of the system. In the past, the only concern was to minimize the downtime of maintenance crews.

The adoption of EVA coincided with a decision by Montana Power to sell its electric generating assets in Montana, which include five coal-fired plants and 13 dams with a book value of $600 million. As a monopoly distributor of electricity in its franchise area, Montana Power doesn't relish the prospect of being the only electric generator in its area still under the boot of regulation. In addition, electric generation is becoming a much riskier business, a capital-intensive enterprise whose deregulated prices rise and fall in step with volatile oil and gas prices. "The competitive electric-generating business is significantly different from the regulated business we have known," says chairman Robert P. Gannon. "Its rapidly changing nature provides a very different risk/reward situation, with more risk than fits our business strategy." Montana Power had been thinking about exiting the generating business for some time, and EVA analysis confirmed the wisdom of the move.

No telephone company anywhere faces tougher competition than Telecom New Zealand, which has to do battle with 10 of the world's 20 largest telecommunications companies in a market of just 3.5 million people. Any sympathy, however, should be reserved for the interlopers. In the years since economist Roderick Deane became CEO at the end of 1992, Telecom has slashed costs and prices, vastly expanded its product offerings, and created more shareholder wealth relative to its capital base than all but a handful of its counterparts around the world.

The transformation of Telecom actually began in the mid-1980s and was part of a total remaking of the New Zealand economy. After decades of socialist policies had brought the island country to near bankruptcy, New Zealand did an astounding about-face and embraced free-market capitalism, with dazzling results. Over the course of several years, New Zealand "corporatized" all of the commercial functions that had been carried out by government—a process that Roderick Deane oversaw—and began opening all its markets, from telephone service to air traffic control, to competition. When Telecom was broken out of the Post Office and corporatized in 1987, it was a model of socialist inefficiency. Customers had to wait two to three months to get a phone installed, equipment was antiquated, it could be all but impossible to place a trunk call from Wellington to Auckland during peak business hours, and it took a staff of 1,000 people five months to process the bills for domestic toll calls.

Telecom was privatized in 1990, with Ameritech and Bell Atlantic buying a controlling interest. Most of its service problems had been resolved by late 1992, but the company still operated with "the attitude of a monopoly in a dormant climate," as Deane puts it. Revenues were declining and the company plainly was on a going-out-of-business trajectory; it was losing market share in domestic and international toll calls at the astounding rate of one percentage point a month. That's when the board recruited Deane to take over as CEO. His first step was to match the competition on prices, which stopped the loss of market share in domestic toll calls in three months and international calls in six. Deane persuaded Bennett McMillen, a recently retired Bell Atlantic executive, to serve as chief operating officer for a few years and bring service up to world-class standards, and recruited Jeff White from Ameritech as CFO.

Deane and White proceeded to introduce an informal version of EVA. "It was basically an EVA approach," Deane says. "The planning process was built around how do you grow this company? How do you get the revenues growing? How do you get the costs down? And how do you economize on capital?" Telecom began to measure EVA in what Deane calls "a rough and ready way" and introduced a form of EVA bonuses for senior managers. Capital spending dropped in those early years from $700 million to $400 million, and then moved back upward as Deane began investing $120 million a year and more in software to automate things like that billing system, which now employs just 60 people and posts toll charges to customer accounts almost instantaneously. (All figures for Telecom are in New Zealand dollars.)

"I felt that a few of us at the senior level basically thought automatically in terms of EVA without actually knowing about all the work Stern Stewart had done on the subject," says Deane. "What I was gradually trying to do was formalize the number crunching and get it cascading through the company." In 1994 Deane concluded that Telecom needed a complete EVA system, with uncapped bonuses and a bonus bank, to move capital discipline and an entrepreneurial spirit throughout the company. Telecom executives say the transition was predictably difficult for some company veterans, especially in the main telephone network operation, but nearly all of them came around when they saw that Deane would settle for nothing less. "EVA didn't really come to the forefront of people's minds," says Chris Rutledge, manager of human resources, "until Roderick said, 'When you come to see me, I want you to tell me what your EVA drivers are.' Then we had a run on the EVA manuals."

Telecom put the 150 most senior managers on EVA incentives in April 1995. As part of the changeover to EVA bonuses, the company required the managers to sign new employment agreements. Rutledge expected that as many as one-third would decline, but all of them signed up for EVA. A year later, Telecom extended the incentives to another 600 managers. "This year is our fourth with the EVA program and EVA today is accepted as part of how we do business," says Rutledge. "It is integral to our reward, planning, analysis, and reporting processes."

The first big changes came in working-capital management and capital appropriations. "Without EVA we would still be hitting down the high resource-consumption path," says David de Boer, who served in the financial performance group during the EVA implementation. "We would have ended up with a bigger balance sheet, more capital employed, and we would have a lot more people in the business." Instead, total employment has dropped from 27,000 at the time of corporatization to around 8,500. De Boer adds that the telephone network group used to invest in technology for its own sake, but under EVA has been responding to market demands. "People basically are quite smart," says de Boer. "It's how you direct their smarts that really counts at the end of the day."

One of the actions Deane took, which had a profound impact on attitudes in the network group, was the realization of an economist's dream. In the spring of 1996 he broke out the network hardware group into a stand-alone business unit called Connected. Now the field forces decide what they need to meet their strategic goals and contract with Connected to do the work. That's fairly common nowadays, but what is uncommon at Telecom is that the operating units have the choice of going outside the company for services if they can get a better price, and Connected can sell its services to competitors. This is a transfer-pricing arrangement that economists specializing in organizational theory have been recommending for decades, but scarcely any corporations have had the courage to adopt.

In the investment area, EVA dissuaded Telecom from participating in a number of joint ventures across the Pacific Rim. "We looked at India and Indonesia and Vietnam and the Philippines and places like that," says Deane. "We were invited by a number of players to join them as partners in those countries. But when we really ran the numbers down on an EVA basis, the payoff period was 20 to 30 years out, and the risks looked too high. Others were prepared to make those investments. They might've made the right judgment, but I've been more worried about performing well than I have about just being big." Telecom certainly has been performing well under Deane. The market value of the company's stock has gone from $4 billion in the spring of 1993 to $14 billion five years later. Telecom's total return to investors has been the highest among major New Zealand companies, and it has created the most MVA—$2.60—per dollar of invested capital.

The first New Zealand company to adopt EVA, in 1992, was Airways Corporation. That is the unlikely name of the nation's air-traffic control operation, which was corporatized in the eighties reform. Airways Corporation also had the distinction of being the first state-owned enterprise (SOE) to pay a dividend to the New Zealand Treasury, and the first corporation anywhere to publish a full accounting of its EVA financial statements in its annual report—and it put them *ahead* of the GAAP income statement and balance sheet. The move to EVA came at the instigation of the then CEO, Andrew Makin, and Stuart Wilson, who was finance director at the time and is now manager of the commercial group.

The new performance measure initially encountered resistance at the board level, but the directors were soon won over. One reason they warmed to EVA is that it helped solve a difficult political problem. The Treasury had complained that Airways was underpricing its services to airlines, while the airlines claimed they were being gouged. EVA gave Airways a way to make both sides happy. It now sets prices to achieve zero EVA over a period of several years (that is, to fully recover its cost of capital, but nothing more), a practice that assures the Treasury that it is getting a fair return on the taxpayers' investment while proving to the airlines that they aren't being overcharged. Airways employees also took to EVA, especially when management put them on EVA incentives. "It's a fun place," says Wilson. "People are motivated. They believe there's trust in them, and that they will share in the rewards, and people respond."

EVA was so successful at Airways that Transpower, the state-owned enterprise that runs New Zealand's electricity distribution, adopted it as well. By 1996 Airways and Transpower were doing so well, and returning such nice dividends to the Treasury, that the government ordered the 15 other SOEs to begin reporting their results and plans, and estimates of their market values, on an EVA basis.

Incredible as it may seem to those who haven't been paying close attention, the U.S. Postal Service may be one of the greatest EVA success stories anywhere. The Postal Service has been structured much like a New Zealand SOE since 1971, when Congress ended its status as a government department and made it an "independent entity of the executive branch." Ever since, the Postal Service was supposed to have operated like a private corporation with an independent board of governors, pricing its services to break even on an accounting basis and without subsidies from the Treasury. Instead, it ran up accumulated losses of $9 billion from fiscal 1972 through fiscal 1994 and seemed utterly immune to improvement through private-sector management practices.

The Postal Service's adoption of EVA began in the fall of 1993, when Sam Winters, vice chairman of the board of governors, sent a *FORTUNE* cover story on EVA to Postmaster General Marvin Runyon and CFO Michael Riley. Runyon, a former vice president of Ford Motor Company and former CEO of Nissan U.S.A., had taken over at the Postal Service the year before after spearheading a major reform of the Tennessee Valley Authority. He was unfamiliar with EVA. Riley, however, had been planning an EVA implementation at his former employer, Lee Enterprises, a newspaper and radio chain, until a new CEO vetoed it; he urged Runyon to go forward. The board of governors agreed, and the implementation began early in 1994.

The timing couldn't have been more propitious. The Postal Service's operating deficit in fiscal 1993, ended September 30 of that year, was its highest ever at $1.8 billion, and service had sunk to a new low as well. The USPS has a "service standard" of delivering 92% of first-class mail to contiguous areas the next day, but its record that year was only 79%. Mail movement in Chicago was virtually paralyzed some of the time, and the overnight delivery performance in most large cities was in the 50% to 60% range. The result was a well-deserved barrage of criticism in Congress and the press.

Implementing any kind of reform at the Postal Service is a daunting proposition. At $58 billion, it had the ninth-highest revenues of all U.S. companies in 1997, its nearly 800,000 employees are the largest civilian workforce in the world, and it is the largest and most complex network organization anywhere. The U.S. Postal Service handles 40% of the world's mail (Japan is second at 8%), and delivers more than 600 million pieces of mail *a day* to 130 million addresses. Before they could set EVA goals for its 10 geographic areas and 85 performance clusters (or PCs), Riley and company had to figure out a cost of capital for the Postal Service. The relevant cost of capital is its most direct competition in the private sector, which one would assume is overnight delivery services such as Federal Express. In fact, overnight and two-day Priority Mail constitutes a minuscule portion of total Postal Service business. Its most significant competition turned out to be the fax machine, so it settled on a 12% cost of capital, which is about average for telecommunications.

The implementation team also had to answer a number of recondite questions, such as how to allocate revenues and costs to measure EVA for the 10 areas and 85 PCs. That issue is horridly complicated by the fact that all the revenue nominally goes to the PC where customers buy stamps or metered postage, while the costs show up at both the "originating" centers where letters and packages are mailed, which isn't always the same place where stamps are bought, and the "destinating" (ugh) centers where letters are sorted and delivered. L. L. Bean, for example, buys its postage in Freeport, Maine, but then trucks its mail-order catalogs to post offices better equipped to handle high-volume processing. What's more, the Postal Service had to deal with considerable political flack from Representative Patricia Schroeder, who accused Runyon and company of hiring "high-priced New York consultants" for the sole purpose of finding a way to circumvent the compensation cap on federal employees, now $151,800. The Postal Service is technically exempt from the compensation ceiling, but adheres to it for obvious political reasons, and bonus payments are cut off when an individual reaches the ceiling.

The Postal Service put 700 top executives on an EVA bonus plan in fiscal 1996, added 61,846 managers and 16,482 supervisors in fiscal 1997, and added another 35,000 employees in fiscal 1998. Riley had hoped to extend bonus payments down to clerks and letter carriers, but their unions balked at the plan. That's unsurprising, since unions instinctively resist incentive plans. It is in the vested interest of any union leadership for members to believe that every gain they get is by dint of the union's efforts rather than their individual performance. Many of the workers themselves, however, are irate over being shut out of the bonus scheme, and Riley still hopes to get universal coverage eventually.

Bonus payments to those in the plan are based 100% on local performance at the PC level, 50% on area EVA and 50% on national EVA at the area level, and 100% on national EVA for most of those at headquarters. The bonuses also hinge on meeting three categories of service goals that fall under the bizarre titles of Voice of the Customer, Voice of the Employee, and Voice of the Business. Positive EVA is a Voice of the Business goal, improved safety performance is a Voice of the Employee goal, and such things as the standard of 92% overnight delivery within contiguous areas is a Voice of the Customer goal. Without the service requirements, employees would have an incentive to give short shrift to customers in order to meet financial goals.

The Postal Service's results since implementing the new system have been downright stunning. It posted profits of $1.8 billion in fiscal 1995 (the highest ever), $1.6 billion in 1996, and $1.3 billion in 1997. The 1995 profit was unremarkable because of a postal rate increase that year, but the Postal Service has always slipped into deficit by the second year following an increase; this was the first time it ever had three consecutive years in the black. The 1997 profit was especially surprising; Riley himself had budgeted a profit of just $55 million for the year. Shortly after the year ended, he told a group of Postal Service executives: "I thought we would slip through with a small profit in 1997. Where did you go right and where did I go wrong? I think I went wrong by underestimating your response to the pay incentives of EVA."

The financial success alone would be impressive, but it also has been accompanied by significant improvements in service. New York City is a case in point. In fiscal 1994, the New York performance cluster achieved overnight delivery on only 52% of first-class letters, but was up to 92% by 1997. "With EVA," says Vinnie E. Malloy, manager of the processing and distribution centers, "people understand that if you don't meet goals it impacts their bonuses." The New York operation achieved its signal improvement while simultaneously cutting one million work hours between 1994 and 1997. It also came in $24 million under budget in 1997. "We underspent our budget," says Malloy. "In effect, we gave back money. That's unusual for a bureaucracy."

Malloy says the improvement came from consolidating all processing of outgoing mail in a single plant and replacing old sorting machines that were slow and had high error rates. Malloy, who oversees four processing plants in New York, started as a distribution clerk 28 years ago and worked her way up the ranks. "We are reducing work hours even more and want to go under budget this year by becoming more efficient, increasing productivity, reducing overtime, and adding more new equipment," she says. "We want to get a better return on our investment every year. It's not just about money. It's about pride. We get paid well to do these jobs and this is the way we should operate. We should be compared to corporate America, not the government."

The Postal Service plans to achieve continuous improvement by extending individual initiatives throughout the system. One of those is a "revenue assurance" project that governor Sam Winters suggested. This basically involves going through old records and collecting unpaid bills or correcting bills that originally were invoiced at too low a rate. The Postal Service put its first revenue assurance analysts into the field in January 1997 and collected $20 million by that September. Steve Andrzejezyk, head of the program, says he had 104 agents across the country in fiscal 1998 with a goal of $100 million of collections for the year. Much of the uncollected postage has come from government agencies, including the Department of Agriculture and the Internal Revenue Service. The problem wasn't that the agencies are deadbeats. Rather, the Postal Service had neglected to bill them in the first place. This year the assurance agents also are looking at past billings to magazine publishers and nonprofit organizations, some of which may have claimed larger discounts than they were entitled to for bulk mailings.

A change in operating procedures in Salt Lake City is typical of the new thinking within the Postal Service. The Salt Lake City processing and distribution facility had been operating on a 24-hour schedule, with the result that operations and maintenance personnel had to compete for time to use the equipment and to maintain, repair, and clean it. As a result, equipment broke down regularly, reducing the overall efficiency of the facility. In March 1997 Sam Ruden, then the plant manager, and Gus Chaus, now acting manager, came up with a system under which the sorting crews work only from 1 P.M. to 7:30 A.M., leaving 5.5 hours a day for maintenance. "EVA drove us to step back and think outside the box," says Chaus. "We operate the plant more efficiently in that reduced time window." The change lowered operating expenses by $5 million. Steve Juhl, finance manager for the Western area in Denver, was so impressed that he ordered up a feasibility study for similar changes at other plants in the area. "Salt Lake City was our most successful performance cluster in fiscal 1997," he says, "and a direct contribution came from the reduction of the operating window."

A working capital initiative in Albuquerque in fiscal 1997 proved so successful that it is being copied by other processing centers in the Western area. Charles Davis, the Albuquerque district manager, spearheaded a critical evaluation of all nonpersonnel expenditures. "Expenditure overruns had plagued this district since it was formed in 1992," says Davis. "We found that we were buying in quantities that we didn't need and buying some items that we didn't need at all." The district trained its purchasing agents, postmasters, and station officials in a system that enables it to track purchases at the performance cluster level, and persuaded the Topeka supply center to change its software so it could track inventories better. "Because of that effort," says Davis, "we were able to get our expenditures $4.7 million under budget. The bottom line was that our total operating expenditures were the sixth-best out of the 85 performance clusters.

We had never made the top 50 before." Still, Albuquerque reached only 82% of its 1997 EVA goal. "That is not acceptable," says Davis. "We want 100% of EVA payout. We're going for everything. We want to define our success by 100% EVA." Meanwhile, the Western area has mandated that all its performance clusters adopt the Albuquerque tracking system.

The experience at the Postal Service differs from that of most corporations in one significant way. Usually, companies adopting EVA find that they have been woefully inefficient in their use of capital and have overinvested in many areas. The situation at the Postal Service was the exact opposite. It had used an excessively high 20% hurdle rate for capital spending, and had underinvested in up-to-date sorting equipment. Many of the improvements across the system, like those in New York, have come from increased capital spending on equipment that is returning far more than the system's 12% cost of capital. Says CFO Riley, summing up the experience of the past three years: "I think none of the success the Postal Service has had would have been possible if we hadn't first picked EVA as a financial measure and an incentive system. We needed something that could withstand the inevitable political attacks and that had worked dramatically in the private sector. It was the key to getting us rolling."

11

Closing the GAAP between Earnings and EVA

The accounting profession has labored mightily for the past quarter century to make income statements and balance sheets more accurately reflect the performance and financial condition of corporations. The Financial Accounting Standards Board, the profession's self-regulatory body, has issued more than 100 new rules, many of them numbingly complex, since it replaced the old Accounting Principles Board in 1973. But instead of improving the product, all this toil and trouble by the auditing overseers has moved generally accepted accounting principles farther and farther away from economic reality. As Baruch Lev, a prominent accounting professor at New York University, sums up the matter in one of his many studies of accounting distortions: "The association between accounting data and market values is not only weak, but appears to have been deteriorating over time. Overall, the fragile association between accounting data and capital market values suggests that the usefulness of financial reports . . . is rather limited."

The widening gap, as it were, between GAAP and reality grows out of an extreme conservative bias in the accounting profession. When accountants are faced with a choice of several ways to treat an item, they almost invariably choose the option that will put the smallest number on the income statement or balance sheet. They immediately charge off all spending on intangibles such as research and development and employee training even though companies make those investments only because they expect a positive return in the future. Companies that extend credit to customers have to take a charge against earnings for bad-debt losses the instant they make new loans. Some borrowers will default, of course, but most will not. In measuring performance, which is what earnings purport to do, immediately booking losses equal to the percentage of loans that are likely to go bad makes no more sense than immediately booking profits on the rest.

Accountants have plenty of reasons to be conservative, of course. Historically, they have prepared their statements primarily for use by lenders, whose concerns are very different from those of owners and managers. Lenders care much less about profitability and performance than they do about whether they can get their hands on enough stuff to recover their loans if a borrower goes bust. As a result, accounting statements provide a portrait of a company from an undertaker's point of view. Balance sheets, after all the writing down of assets and reserving for possible future expenses, do not provide a measure of the cash that investors have put at risk in a going concern, or what we call capital. Instead, they come much closer to showing the minimum amount that a liquidator could expect to get for the assets in a fire sale.

The securities laws are another important contributor to this abject conservatism. When accountants get sued for securities fraud, it is for *over*stating earnings or assets, not understating them, so their self-interest is solidly on the side of debiting earnings. In addition, the Securities and Exchange Commission, which is the final arbiter of accounting rules for publicly held corporations, has mandated some of the more foolish provisions in GAAP. It was the SEC, for example, that insisted on the requirement that companies amortize goodwill. The SEC makes these rules out of an abiding fear that shady managers will hornswoggle investors by inflating earnings and assets. The rich history of stock swindles may justify such fears, but the SEC's protective zeal sometimes takes it to absurd extremes. One case in point: Back in the 1970s the SEC became concerned that naive investors were being misled by the emphasis that real estate investment trusts put on cash flow, so it ordered all companies to stop reporting cash flow per share. All were still required to report cash flow and the number of shares outstanding, of course. The threat to the fairness of the markets apparently came from allowing companies to perform the long division for their shareholders.

Finally, the distortions caused by accounting conservatism have been exacerbated by changes in the nature of business over the past few decades. As Baruch Lev points out, a big culprit in the weakening association between financial statements and reality is the "frequent contamination of [earnings] by transitory and arbitrary items, such as asset write-offs, restructuring charges, goodwill amortization, and the full expensing of research and development." "Arbitrary" refers, of course, to accounting treatments, not business actions. All these areas are ones in which accountants are far too eager to reduce earnings and balance sheets, which means that GAAP is particularly ill-suited to the business environment that is likely to prevail in the coming decades.

Quantum erring on the side of caution may or may not serve creditors well (a strong case can be made that it often does not), but GAAP plainly fails to meet the needs of managers and shareholders. These optimistic folk rightly view the corporation not as a candidate for interment, but as an enterprise that will continue in operation into the indefinite future and hopefully will provide a handsome return. What they need is a performance measure that provides signals and feedback that confirm or refute the wisdom of capital allocation decisions and serves as a reliable guide to the economic value of a company. Managers in particular need a performance metric that shows, month to month and quarter to quarter, whether their actions are adding to the value of the business. To achieve that, they do not need liquidation values or even the fair market value of assets. Rather, they need a balance sheet that provides a measure of the cumulative cash outlays expected to contribute to future profits, which constitutes the proper capital base on which to measure rates of return and EVA. They also need a corresponding measure of operating profits that reflects what really is happening in the business.

That's precisely what EVA provides. Companies cannot replace GAAP earnings with EVA in their public reporting, of course. But no regulations prevent them from using a different earnings calculation for internal decisions, or from reporting that number to investors alongside the one mandated by the SEC. The first departure from GAAP accounting is to recognize the full cost of capital. Accountants treat equity as if it were free. EVA also fixes the problems with GAAP by converting accounting earnings to economic earnings and accounting book value to economic book value, or capital. The result is a NOPAT figure (net operating profits after taxes) that gives a much truer picture of the economics of the business, and a capital figure that is a far better measure of the funds contributed by shareholders and lenders.

The first step in calculating EVA for any one company is to decide on which adjustments to make to the GAAP accounts. As you will see, the correct answer usually is far fewer than you might expect, though one could make EVA overly complicated by insisting on a plethora of unnecessary accounting adjustments. Stern Stewart, for example, has identified more than 160 potential adjustments to GAAP and to internal accounting treatments, all of which can improve the measure of operating profits and capital. Any change in the accounting adjustments will yield a different EVA number, of course. If you think of all the potential EVAs as running along a spectrum (see Figure 11.1), the one at the extreme left is what might be called "basic" EVA. This is the EVA you would get using unadjusted GAAP operating profits and the GAAP balance sheet. Moving to the right, you come to what we call "disclosed" EVA. This EVA, which Stern Stewart uses in its published MVA/EVA rankings, is computed

Figure 11.1

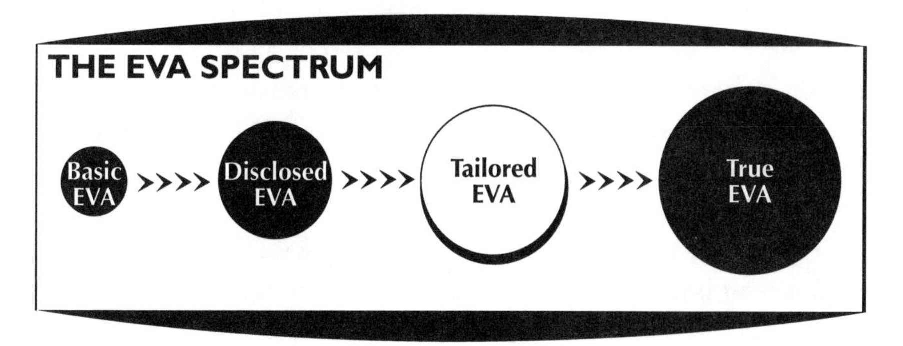

by making about a dozen standard adjustments to publicly available accounting data. At the extreme right is "true" EVA. This is the most theoretically correct and accurate measure of economic profit, calculated with all relevant adjustments to accounting data and using the precise cost of capital for each business unit in a corporation.

Which EVA should a company use? None of the above. Basic EVA is an improvement on regular accounting earnings because it recognizes that equity capital has a cost, but all the other problems with GAAP remain. At the other extreme, the calculation of true EVA requires more wisdom than mere mortals possess. Disclosed EVA is much, much better than basic EVA. As mentioned in Chapter 5, disclosed EVA explains about 50% of changes in MVA. But disclosed EVA is not as good as it should be for internal management use. That's partly because publicly reported figures do not include enough detail to fine-tune some of the accounting adjustments. It also reflects the fact that some practical shortcuts are inescapable in doing timely EVA computations for large rankings of companies.

In fact, no off-the-shelf definition of EVA will do. What each company needs is a custom-tailored definition, peculiar to its organizational structure, business mix, strategy, and accounting policies—one that optimally balances the trade-off between simplicity (the ease with which it can be calculated and understood) and precision (the accuracy with which it captures true economic profit). These custom-tailored EVAs typically explain 60% to as much as 85% of changes in MVA. In Stern Stewart's experience, most companies require no more than 15 accounting adjustments to calculate an optimal EVA, and many can get by with fewer still. Once the formula is set, it should be virtually immutable, serving as a sort of constitutional definition of performance. Top management and the board should be just as circumspect about fiddling with their chosen EVA as Congress is about amending the U.S. Constitution.

The myriad formulas for EVA may make it sound rather muddy and easily manipulated, and some commentators have cited this as a serious shortcoming. Professors Israel Shaked and Allen Michel of Boston University, writing in *Strategy & Business*, complain that "companies can pick and choose among the multitude of possible adjustments, creating something of a free-for-all in the metrics marketplace, a situation that awaits a regulatory referee to sort out." Nonsense. Flexibility and customizability are important strengths of EVA, not weaknesses. The purpose, after all, isn't to arrive at some theoretically pristine measure of profits. Rather, it is to change the behavior of managers and workers in ways that will maximize shareholder wealth, and the effectiveness of any measure in shaping behavior will diminish as it becomes more complex and difficult to understand. Since particular accounting adjustments may be crucial in some industries and unimportant in others, tailoring allows each company to limit its adjustments to those that are truly necessary. Some competing measures of corporate performance, including cash flow return on investment (CFROI), start out exceedingly complicated and can never be made simple enough for even the smartest nonfinancial managers to comprehend. EVA, in contrast, starts out simple and gets only as complicated as it has to be to provide the right information for managers and workers to make wealth-maximizing decisions. But again, once the definition has been decided on, it should not be modified lightly.

The list of potential accounting changes is too lengthy to detail here. The various types of adjustments include the treatment of such things as: the timing of expense and revenue recognition; passive investments in marketable securities; securitized assets and other off-balance-sheet financing; restructuring charges; inflation; foreign currency translation; inventory valuation; bookkeeping reserves; bad-debt recognition; intangible assets; taxes; pensions; postretirement expenses; marketing expenditures; goodwill and other acquisition issues; and strategic investments. Some adjustments are necessary to avoid mixing operating and financing decisions. Some provide a long-term perspective. Some avoid mixing stocks and flows. Some convert GAAP accrual items to a cash-flow basis, while others convert GAAP cash-flow items to additions to capital. Still others, including overhead allocations and transfer pricing issues, change internal accounting treatments to resolve organizational interface problems that distort decisions. The following examples include some of the major adjustments necessary to put NOPAT and capital on an economic basis, and further illuminate ways that GAAP distorts reality in these areas:

- Research and development
- Strategic investments
- Accounting for acquisitions
- Expense recognition
- Depreciation
- Restructuring charges
- Taxes
- Balance sheet adjustments

Research and development. The treatment of R&D provides an excellent example of the difference between accounting and economics. As noted earlier, shareholders and managers rightly regard outlays on R&D as investments in future products and processes. GAAP, however, requires companies (software developers are the signal exception) to immediately expense (deduct from earnings) all outlays for research and development. GAAP is saying, in effect, that the more than $100 billion a year that U.S. corporations invest in research and development is worthless. This punitive treatment of R&D has particularly perverse consequences for research-intensive high-tech companies. Expensing R&D wrongly reduces their book values by writing one of their greatest assets down to zero. A principal reason that high-tech stocks typically sell at much higher multiples of book value than other companies is that their book values are so egregiously understated.

The EVA treatment is to capitalize R&D investments (add current outlays to the balance sheet as an asset) and amortize them (charge a portion against earnings each year) over an appropriate period. Research by Baruch Lev and others indicates that the correct amortization period ranges from as little as three or four years for scientific instruments to eight years or more for pharmaceuticals. The average useful life of R&D for all industries is five years, which is the amortization period that Stern Stewart uses in the Performance 1000. All companies with significant R&D spending should capitalize it. Why? Because the adjustment can occasionally have a material impact on decisions. A CEO playing by the rules according to GAAP might order a cutback in R&D spending in a lean year in order to bolster earnings, even though that means the company is sacrificing shareholder wealth by forgoing an investment that promises to return more than the cost of capital. (If the R&D isn't likely to return more than the cost of capital, the company shouldn't have been doing it in the first place.) Alternatively, the CEO might be reluctant to increase spending to capture a first-strike advantage in a promising technology area.

Research indicates that the GAAP treatment of R&D has pernicious effects even in normal years. Robert Gibbons of Cornell University and Kevin J. Murphy of Harvard studied R&D spending patterns in the final years before CEOs retire. R&D doesn't decline, but the rate of increase in R&D does. Gibbons and Murphy believe that CEOs whose pensions are based on earnings performance in their final years on the job become stingy with R&D dollars to pad their own pensions. The findings also indicate that the CEOs in question understand what they are doing to shareholders. The falloff in R&D is significantly smaller when CEOs hold substantial amounts of stock or options, the value of which would be reduced by curtailing R&D.

Under EVA, and with bonuses and pensions based on EVA instead of earnings, the CEO would not face such destructive temptations; cutting R&D outlays would have no immediate impact on EVA. But, and this is also important, the amortization of R&D in future years makes managers feel accountable for getting results. In too many companies, R&D is simply institutionalized at a certain spending level precisely because it is treated as an expense. When R&D is treated as an investment, the system automatically creates more leeway to increase spending on an attractive project, while the charge for the cost of capital and accountability under the EVA bonus system ensure that researchers appraise prospective projects objectively.

Strategic investments. Capital discipline is the essence of EVA, but there are times when companies do not want managers to worry about covering their full cost of capital—at least not immediately. These are the instances when the payoff from an investment is not expected to come until some point in the future. Managers at a forest products company, for example, see great potential in a new, more efficient pulp mill that would take three years to construct and bring up to full capacity. But they may be reluctant to propose it because they know that their EVA will be reduced by capital charges imposed on the new investment before the mill begins to produce profits.

The same disincentive to investment can dissuade companies from making wealth-creating acquisitions. Monsanto, which implemented EVA in 1996, has completed a number of acquisitions over the past couple of years as it spun off its chemical business and refocused itself as a "life sciences" company with extensive operations in food, agriculture, and pharmaceuticals. Chief executive Robert B. Shapiro would have rejected many of those acquisitions if the test had been whether they would immediately contribute to higher EVA. But Monsanto has not been acquiring just to round out the offerings in its catalogs. Instead, it has been buying biotech companies whose research will help Monsanto develop more breakthrough products. The EVA payoff will come down the road as the products move from development to market. Similarly, most upscale restaurants operate at a loss—or too small an operating profit to cover the interest on the initial investment in fixtures and kitchen equipment—until they build a loyal customer base, something that rarely happens overnight.

The approach that many non-EVA companies take in situations like these is to define the investments as strategic and basically ignore the immediate impact on profitability. This has great appeal for everyone (except the shareholders) because it is essentially discipline-free. When the time comes for the profits to finally materialize, hardly anyone ever looks back to see if they are as large as promised or large enough to justify the initial investment—which is why so many people have come to regard "strategic" as a code word for a project or acquisition that will never pay off. EVA provides a better way—one that encourages managers to propose investments with distant payoffs, but only when they believe (and don't just hope) that the investment will return more than the cost of capital.

The solution is to use a special accounting treatment for strategic investments that is akin to the construction-in-progress accounting used by electric utilities. Instead of applying a capital charge to strategic investments from the day they are made, EVA companies "hold back" the investment in a special "suspension" account. The capital charge on the balance in the suspension account is left out of the EVA calculation until the time that the investment is expected to produce operating profits. In the interim, the capital charges that would have been applied to the suspension account are simply added to it, so that the balance in the account reflects the full opportunity cost—including accrued interest, as it were—of the investment. Then, when the investment is scheduled to begin producing NOPAT, the capital in the suspension account is metered back into the EVA calculation.

This is strategic investment with a memory. The strategic investment treatment stretches out managers' horizons and encourages them to consider opportunities with distant payoffs. Managers proposing investments understand that they will not be penalized in the short term for taking a long-term view, but also know that they ultimately will be held accountable for the capital invested. However, as with the EVA formula itself, it is essential that companies establish the rules for strategic treatment in advance and then stick to them.

Accounting for acquisitions. When one company acquires another and uses the purchase method of accounting to record the transaction, anything it pays in excess of the "fair value" of the acquired company's assets goes on its balance sheet as an asset called goodwill. Arithmetically, goodwill is simply purchase price minus "fair value." Economically, it could represent any number of things. Goodwill may include the value of patents, technological know-how, or R&D projects that are still in process. And some part of goodwill may be exactly what the name implies: the goodwill that the acquired company and its brands have established with customers and suppliers.

Whatever its true source, goodwill is an intangible, and accountants get very uncomfortable around things they can't touch. So GAAP requires companies to write off goodwill over a period of 40 years or less. This treatment of goodwill plays havoc with the information content in accounting numbers. The annual amortization charge arbitrarily reduces reported earnings, which also reduces conventional profitability measures such as return on equity (ROE) and return on assets (ROA). Ultimately, however, the accumulated amortization charges reduce equity and assets so far that the treatment of goodwill inflates ROE and ROA.

That's just the beginning of the mischief. Since 1970 GAAP has required acquirers to allocate an appropriate share of the purchase price to "identifiable" intangible assets, including R&D. In recent years acquirers have been doing just that by estimating, sometimes with the help of outside appraisers, the market value of in-process R&D. They aren't doing this just to be in compliance with the 1970 accounting rule. Their real motivation is to single out the R&D portion of goodwill *so they can write it off immediately*. When IBM bought Lotus Development Corporation for $3.2 billion in 1995, for example, it allocated $1.84 billion, or 57% of the purchase price, to in-process R&D. IBM then wrote off the entire amount under the GAAP rule requiring companies to expense R&D. Why jump through these hoops? Because immediately writing off the in-process R&D gets a big chunk of goodwill off the books now, which reduces ongoing goodwill amortization charges and boosts reported earnings. The write-off also puts more zing in ROE and ROA by immediately shrinking shareholders' equity and assets.

Baruch Lev calls this the "flash-then-flush" maneuver. The acquirer flashes the estimated market value of acquired R&D to shareholders and then flushes it off the balance sheet. Interestingly, Lev's examination of nearly 400 instances in which acquirers used flash-then-flush shows that the estimated market values of the in-process R&D correlated highly with the stock market valuations of the acquiring companies. Lev's research also provides an empirical validation of the EVA treatment of R&D. He found that the valuations that acquirers put on in-process R&D were close to the book values that the R&D would have had using the EVA approach of capitalizing and amortizing outlays.

The proper economic treatment of goodwill is to write it off over its estimated economic life. For three practical reasons, Stern Stewart recommends leaving goodwill on the balance sheet and never writing it off. First, this focuses managers on cash flows rather than mere bookkeeping entries. Second, most goodwill represents assets with indefinite lives, such as brands, reputation, and market position. Finally, managers shouldn't be concerned about how a prospective acquisition will affect reported earnings, but they should be constantly aware that shareholders will expect them to produce a return on the acquisition price that equals or exceeds the cost of capital *in perpetuity*. Thus, the EVA adjustment is to add the current period's goodwill amortization back to NOPAT and to add the goodwill amortized in past years back to capital.

Pooling-of-interest acquisitions present an entirely different set of problems. In these cases, the balance sheets of the two companies are simply added together and goodwill isn't accounted for at all. The absence of goodwill means there are no ongoing amortization charges to penalize reported earnings. This makes poolings very attractive to managers of acquiring companies; so attractive, as mentioned before, that they are willing to pay higher acquisition premiums than companies using purchase accounting. However, the pooling treatment, which values acquired companies at accounting book value instead of the normally higher acquisition price, distorts EVA because it understates capital and the capital charge. Thus, the proper EVA treatment is to convert pooling acquisitions to purchase accounting so that managers will focus on the true capital costs of an acquisition.

Expense recognition. Some companies should make changes in things as basic as when they recognize revenues and expenses. Many companies willingly incur marketing costs to establish new brands, enter new markets, or gain market share. America Online, for example, must have sent 20 or 30 disks to access its service to every personal computer owner in the United States. Similarly, cellular telephone companies typically spend $250 to $300 to acquire a new customer, both by selling cellular phones far below cost and by paying finder's fees to telephone retailers. All these outlays are investments to acquire new assets called customers. Yet GAAP accounting says they must be treated as current period expenses and deducted from earnings immediately. Thus, the more successful a cellular company is at landing new subscribers, the less profitable it appears. But is it less profitable? What the cellular company has done is acquire a subscriber who is going to run up monthly charges. If cellular companies capitalized customer acquisition costs and amortized them over the appropriate period, which is the proper economic treatment, their earnings and book values would be much higher. More important, a growing company would not have any reason to cut back on profitable marketing outlays just to make a quarterly earnings number look better.

Depreciation. For most companies, the straight-line depreciation of plant and equipment used in GAAP accounting works acceptably well. While straight-line depreciation doesn't attempt to match the actual economic depreciation of physical assets, the deviations from reality ordinarily are so inconsequential that they do not distort decisions. That's not true, however, for companies with significant amounts of long-lived equipment. In those cases, using straight-line depreciation in calculating EVA can create a powerful bias against investments in new equipment. That's because the EVA capital charge declines in step with the depreciated carrying value of the asset, so that old assets look much cheaper than new ones. This can make managers reluctant to replace "cheap" old equipment with "expensive" new gear.

Companies with long-lived equipment can eliminate this distortion by replacing straight-line depreciation with sinking-fund depreciation. Under a sinking fund schedule, the annual depreciation charge follows the same pattern as the principal payment in a mortgage, starting out small in the early years and rising rapidly in the last years. The sum of the depreciation charge and the EVA capital charge remain constant from year to year, just like a mortgage payment. The switch to sinking-fund depreciation, which effectively makes owning an asset look just like leasing, eliminates any bias against new equipment. It also happens to be much closer to economic reality. Most long-lived equipment depreciates very little in the first few years, and then tumbles in value in the later years when obsolescence and physical deterioration gang up on it.

Restructuring charges. Nothing in GAAP provides worse signals to managers than the treatment of restructuring charges. To see this, think about what a restructuring charge represents. In the GAAP view, the charge is a belated recognition of the loss on an investment that went bad. This has some intellectual merit, but it doesn't capture the dynamics of a restructuring from a managerial perspective. Viewed from the executive suite, a restructuring should be thought of as a redeployment of capital that is intended to improve profitability going forward by reducing the ongoing losses from past mistakes. The GAAP treatment focuses entirely on the past mistakes aspect, and turns a restructuring into a painful mea culpa that most managers would do anything to avoid. The EVA treatment focuses on the likely improvement in shareholder wealth, turning restructurings into opportunities that managers should be eager to seize.

Consider this example of a highly simplified company with a $500 factory that produces zero operating profits. That's breakeven under GAAP, but much worse under EVA. If the company's cost of capital is 10%, the capital charge for the factory is $50 and, with zero operating profits, EVA is minus $50. The company could sell the factory and distribute the proceeds to shareholders, but would get only $200 for it. Under GAAP, the company reports a $300 restructuring charge for the loss on the sale of the factory, which is treated as a $300 reduction in earnings. The balance sheet declines by $500 as the asset is fully written off, and the $200 dividend is paid to shareholders. Few managers who focus on earnings would close the plant. Why take a $300 hit to earnings, a $500 reduction in assets, and a shrinkage in operations if you can continue breaking even under GAAP?

Look at the same situation under EVA. The company takes the $500 factory off its books. But instead of flowing a $300 restructuring charge through the income statement, it adds a $300 restructuring investment to the balance sheet. Capital declines not by $500, but by the $200 actually paid to shareholders from the sale of the factory. This, after all, is the amount of capital management actually returned to shareholders. Now look at what happens to EVA: Operating profits remain at zero (since the factory no longer is operating), but the capital charge drops to $30 (10% of the $300 restructuring investment), and EVA rises from minus $50 to minus $30. A manager whose bonus was based on changes in EVA would sell the factory in a New York minute.

Taxes. The mismeasurement of taxes arises because companies calculate their pretax profits one way for shareholders and a second way for the Internal Revenue Service. The profit—and tax liability—they report to the IRS usually is much lower. Depreciation is the biggest difference between the two sets of books, but not the only one. Companies use accelerated depreciation of fixed assets in computing taxable profits for the IRS and a slower depreciation schedule (usually straight-line) in the profits they report to shareholders. The provision for income taxes used in GAAP earnings statements, commonly referred to as book taxes, isn't the same as the cash taxes companies actually pay. It is the taxes they would owe if they used GAAP earnings on their tax return. The difference—the taxes they don't really pay—goes into a liability account called deferred taxes.

The trouble with this accounting treatment is that most companies never will pay their deferred taxes. Even if a company's fixed assets grow slowly, the depreciation charges on its tax return will keep the deferred tax account rising indefinitely. From an economic standpoint, the only taxes a company should deduct from current earnings are the ones it pays now, not taxes that it might—or might not—have to pay at some distant date. So for the purposes of calculating NOPAT and EVA at the corporate level, companies should deduct only the cash taxes they pay in the period being measured. Correspondingly, the deferred taxes that were deducted from earnings in the past should be moved from the liability portion of the balance sheet and added back to shareholder funds for the purposes of calculating capital and the cost of capital.

Most non-EVA companies use pretax operating profits to evaluate business units, and some EVA companies do so as well. However, most companies should use after-tax NOPAT and EVA at the business-unit level. Since taxes are an inescapable cost of doing business, operating managers should take them into account if they can affect tax liabilities through their decisions. When they are charged for taxes actually paid, managers will have the incentive to collaborate with the tax department at the planning stages of new ventures to determine the most tax-efficient organization instead of calling in the tax experts after the fact to minimize the damage already done by failing to consider taxes until all other decisions had been made.

Balance sheet adjustments. All the adjustments mentioned thus far can have a significant impact on the measurement of capital, or economic book value. Capitalizing R&D and adding back amortized goodwill and tax reserves all add to capital, for example. Several other adjustments that affect the balance sheet directly bear mention. One that many EVA companies make is to subtract passive investments (such as the large cash reserves that some companies hold in marketable securities) because they do not represent capital used to produce operating profits. What's more, passive investments should be valued in the market at the lower cost of capital inherent in the investments themselves rather than at the company's cost of capital. Needless to say, the income on those investments should be subtracted from NOPAT. Another balance sheet adjustment is to subtract the free financing all companies enjoy, which comes in the form of accrued expenses and non-interest-bearing accounts payable. These adjustments limit the capital charge to the net assets employed in operations. Finally, companies should move all off-balance-sheet items, such as uncapitalized leases and securitized receivables, back onto the balance sheet. This is essential to avoid mixing operating and financing decisions. An uncapitalized lease item, for example, will appear cheaper than it really is if managers look only at the implicit lending rate in the lease.

In tailoring EVA to a specific company, Stern Stewart applies a series of tests to determine which accounting adjustments are optimal. The first and most important is whether an adjustment is material. By material, we aren't referring to the accountant's test of whether a number is large relative to a company's earnings or assets. In our world, material means that the numbers involved are significant down at the levels of decision makers even if they cancel out at the corporate level. Material also means that the change in accounting could alter decisions in ways that affect shareholder wealth. If a change cannot affect decisions, it usually isn't worth making.

The other tests of potential adjustments are whether:

- The necessary data are available.
- The change is understandable to operating managers.
- The change can be explained to employees, directors, and stockholders.
- The change is definitive (i.e., the adjustment can be cast in concrete and left unchanged for a minimum of three years).
- The change aligns calculated EVA more closely with the market value of the firm (i.e., the NOPAT calculation is moved closer to economic earnings, and anyone can make the adjustment automatically without any subjective judgments).
- The change involves items that are manageable by those affected.

By manageable, we are referring to whether an operating manager can influence expenses or capital outlays in ways that benefit shareholders. One example is the allocation of corporate overhead, which often is charged to business units on the basis of sales. In those cases, the only way a business unit can affect its allocated overhead expense is by getting sales down, something that presumably is not a good thing for shareholders. The manageability test would dictate that the company either not allocate corporate overhead at all or allocate it according to an activity-based costing formula that a business unit could manage by using fewer corporate services.

The other element in crafting a company's EVA formula is to define the cost of capital. The cost used in all EVA calculations is the weighted average cost of debt and equity capital. This is the percentage of capital provided by lenders multiplied by the company's cost of debt, plus the percentage supplied by shareholders multiplied by the cost of equity capital. That rate, when multiplied by total capital, is the profit that must be earned in order to make interest payments on the debt and leave enough additional profit to provide shareholders with a minimum acceptable return on their investment.

Perhaps the easist way to understand what determines the cost of capital for any company is to divide it into three basic components. The first is the risk-free rate of interest, which usually is measured by the government bond rate. The risk-free interest rate reflects the fact that capital is scarce and that any use of it has a minimum time value, even when the person providing the capital is absolutely certain of getting it all back. The second component of the cost of capital is a premium over the risk-free rate to compensate for business risk. Business risk varies with the level of uncertainty in a company's industry. Food processing, for example, is much less risky than making auto parts or operating theme parks, and the cost of capital for each reflects its relative risk. The third component is a *reduction* in the cost of capital to reflect the savings most companies get from being able to deduct interest payments from their taxable profits, commonly referred to as the tax subsidy on debt. For the vast majority of companies, the sum of the three components comes to a figure that is 1 to 7 percentage points higher than the government bond rate.

What about the separate costs of debt and equity? For the most part, they don't really matter. Apart from the effect of the tax subsidy on debt, the overall cost of capital in a business is purely a function of the underlying business risk and, within reasonable leverage limits, is not affected by the mix of debt and equity. To be sure, the cost of debt is considerably cheaper than equity, for the simple reason that debt holders get paid first. Superficially, it would appear that substituting cheaper debt for more expensive equity is a way to bring down the average cost of capital. However, higher debt gives rise to greater *financial* risk. Shareholders demand to get paid for that type of risk as well. The required return on equity rises as more fixed interest payments are subtracted from uncertain operating profits, making the bottom-line profits available to shareholders riskier or more volatile over a business cycle. One of the contributions that Miller and Modigliani made 40 years ago was to show that, apart from the tax subsidy on debt, the cost of greater financial risk exactly offsets the savings from substituting debt for equity.

In practice, of course, companies do calculate separate costs for debt and equity capital. Debt is simple. It is the company's after-tax cost of borrowing at current interest rates. Current interest rates, rather than the rates on existing debt, are the appropriate ones to use because that is the cost the company would pay on new debt or would save if it repurchased debt. The cost of equity is considerably more complicated. Financial economists and consultants have devised a variety of ways to estimate the cost of equity down to as many decimal places as anyone would like. We each have our preferred method, none of which is worth going into here. Suffice it to say that the differences in estimates produced by the various methodologies usually are less important than the answers to questions about things such as whether to use different costs of capital in different countries, and whether a company should use one cost of capital for every business unit. In answer to the second, Stern Stewart usually recommends using just one cost of capital for the sake of simplicity and ease of administration, and to forestall pointless arguments over the "right" cost. Some cases are exceptions, however, especially when the costs of capital in business units are radically different. Telecom New Zealand, for example, uses one cost of capital for its conventional wired service, and a second, higher one for its wireless phone business.

The specific estimating technique also is much less important for getting the benefits of EVA than the fact that managers explicitly recognize that capital has *some* cost, and their bonuses depend on covering that cost. As with so many other things in business, the calculation of the cost of capital is subject to the 80/20 rule, which says that about 80% of the benefits of determining the right cost come from the first 20% of the effort. Whether the true weighted average cost of capital is 11.5% or 13.2% is of far less importance than having everyone understand that capital is expensive and behave accordingly. Some companies prefer to keep the cost-of-capital issue as simple as possible, figuring that refinement would merely confuse some people without improving decisions. Coca-Cola, for example, uses 12% as its single cost of capital worldwide, expressed in dollars. Why 12%? Because it's 1% a month.

12

SPX: Using EVA and Stretch Goals to Turn a Sputtering Jalopy into a Formula One Winner

Nearly every company adopting EVA quickly finds that years (or even decades) of ineffectual capital management have left it rich in opportunities for immediate performance improvements. Like Quaker Oats at its granola bar factory, many find they can make more profitable trade-offs between inventories and the length of production runs. Others, like Briggs & Stratton, discover that a proper recognition of capital costs suddenly makes outsourcing of some products or components look more attractive. Some find that they have "stuffed" too much output into distribution channels in order to inflate reported earnings. Many become more willing to restructure and dispose of poorly performing assets. And, like Equifax, nearly all companies find ways to reduce working capital by speeding up receivables collections or stretching out payables.

Gathering this low-hanging fruit, so to speak, produces handsome increases in shareholder wealth because most gains from better capital management represent permanent increases in the level of EVA. For a company with a cost of capital of 10%, for example, adding $20 million a year to EVA should boost market value and MVA by some

$200 million. (The formula for estimating the impact on MVA is the permanent improvement in EVA divided by the percentage cost of capital.) However, these are essentially onetime gains, and additional improvements of the same type naturally get harder and harder to come by. Which means that better capital management cannot, by itself, meet the challenge of producing the continuous improvements in EVA that will bring *future* increases in MVA and shareholder wealth.

The only way to continually achieve exceptional increases in EVA is, of course, through growth, and the EVA system can help in a big way here as well. First, the initial onetime gains are more important than they might appear, because they improve a company's competitiveness and enhance its ability to grow profitably. Equally important, EVA incentives provide strong motivation for managers to search out fresh opportunities to grow, since that is the only way they can continually earn outsize bonuses. And the EVA analytical framework is a great aid in separating profitable growth from unprofitable, wealth-destroying growth for its own sake. But truly prodigious growth requires something more than the right performance measure or analytical framework or incentive system. Some business gurus say the key ingredient is a culture of excellence. In *Built to Last*, authors James C. Collins and Jerry I. Porras write about the importance of vision, a sense of corporate mission, and an enduring commitment to core values. Others stress the importance of "breaking the rules" in order to reshape entire industries.

The purpose here is not to assess the merits of various theories about how best to achieve growth. Rather, it is to show how EVA can complement and strengthen growth initiatives. An excellent example in this area is SPX Corporation, a moribund manufacturer of auto parts and specialty automotive tools that suddenly became one of the best-performing companies on the New York Stock Exchange by simultaneously adopting EVA and a high-performance technique known as stretch targeting. Stretch targeting usually is identified with the General Electric Company, which has been using a version of it for nearly a decade. In simplest terms, stretch is a method to increase the probability of achieving breakthroughs in technology, productivity, and growth by setting goals that seemingly are impossible to meet. As John B. Blystone, the CEO of SPX, puts it: "If you know how to get there, it's not stretch. If you can put a probability on achieving it, it's not stretch. And if it is not uncomfortable, it's not stretch."

SPX is the leading producer of so-called essential tools that carmakers require their dealers to use when they perform repairs on cars still under warranty. It also is the leading global administrator of service-equipment programs for franchised car dealers. In addition, SPX makes electronic diagnostic equipment and emissions testing equipment for car dealers and auto service centers, and produces a variety of components for the auto industry, including die-cast steering components and automatic transmission filters. While the company's products generally are regarded as first-rate, its performance in the first half of the nineties was downright dreadful. Profits peaked in the late eighties, went into a tailspin in the 1991 recession, and never really recovered. Earnings per share, for example, were solidly above $2 in the mid eighties, but never got much above $1 in the first half of the nineties, when the company operated in the black in just two years out of five.

Part of the problem was that SPX's 10 operating units functioned more like a loose conglomerate than a family of related businesses. There was a large amount of overlap among the divisions in products and distribution systems, and some even competed with each other, doing duplicate R&D work and driving each other's prices down by bidding aggressively for the same customers. The winner in this destructive combat was rewarded for its "victory" by the head office in Muskegon, Michigan. Some of the division presidents didn't even know each another, something that Blystone found mind-boggling when he arrived at SPX. The one major goal that the company achieved in the first half of the nineties was getting its revenues over the $1 billion mark, which happened in 1994. With that accomplished, the next project was to figure out how to make those revenues consistently profitable. Investors were disdainful of SPX's chances. While the stock market boomed, the price of SPX shares stayed mired in the low teens—or even lower, as in periods like the second quarter of 1995, when the price got down to $10.75 a share.

Management knew it had to do something different, and a coterie in the finance department favored EVA. In the spring of 1995, then-CFO William Trubeck (he later became CFO of International Multifoods, which began implementing EVA in 1997) persuaded Blystone's predecessor to implement EVA. The board of directors ratified the decision, but then forced the CEO out a few months later and began a search for a successor. That December, just as the EVA implementation was nearing completion and senior managers were about to go on EVA incentives, the board hired Blystone, who at the time was chief executive of two GE operations in Italy that had combined revenues three times those of SPX. Blystone had only a passing familiarity with EVA before he arrived in Muskegon, but he quickly warmed to the logic and simplicity of the system, especially the bonus plan.

Blystone set out to fix SPX in a hurry, first by right-sizing and rationalizing operations to make them successful profit generators even in a downturn. The company couldn't embark on ambitious growth plans, he believed, until it fixed what it already had. He also completed a reorganization, begun the year before, that grouped SPX's 10 operating divisions into three main product groups. Most important, he introduced SPX managers to the concept of stretch. Blystone concluded during his first tours of SPX facilities that the managers needed a radical new approach to solving problems and seizing opportunities. "I could see these were good people," he recalls. "But what they were doing was incremental instead of quantum."

During those tours Blystone showed his managers a puzzle that he uses to demonstrate the principle of "thinking outside the box." (See Figures 12.1 and 12.2.) The object of the puzzle is to connect nine dots, grouped in a square like the spaces on a tic-tac-toe board, by drawing four straight lines and without lifting the pencil from the pa-

Figure 12.1

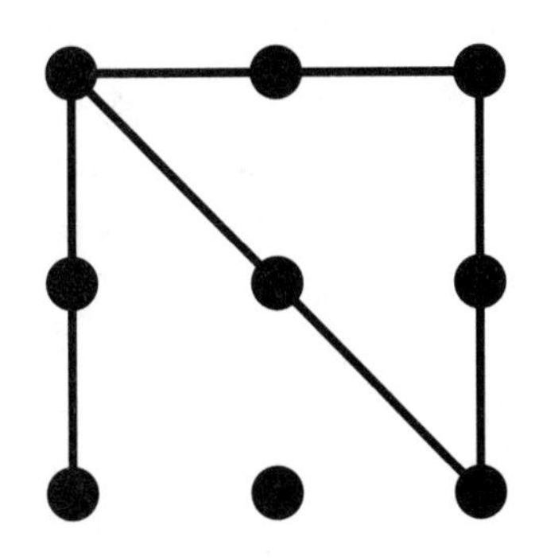

THINKING INSIDE THE BOX

Figure 12.2

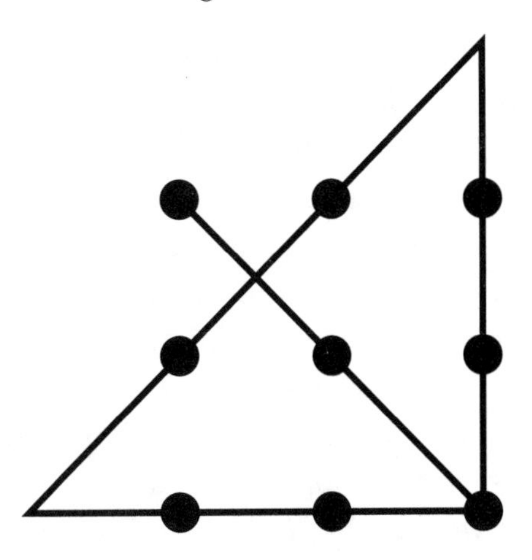

THINKING OUTSIDE THE BOX

per. Most people fail because they do not extend any lines beyond the unseen border of the "box" formed by the dots. The puzzle is easily solved once you realize that there is no rule against using lines that can extend as far outside the box as you like. "When I showed this when I was out touring the business," says Blystone, "people started to think differently, which is what we wanted."

Next came stretch goals, which Blystone introduced in January 1996 at his first meeting of all the divisional executives. As Blystone uses it, stretch—which he also refers to as "thinking quantum"—is about more than just growth; it is the pursuit of dramatic improvement in every dimension of a company's operations. He began by asking what the various operating plans added up to in terms of earnings per share (he was still learning EVA at the time). The answer was $1 a share in earnings from continuing operations, up from 75 cents per share (before restructuring charges) in 1995. A 33% increase might sound good, but it still would have left SPX much less profitable than its main competitors. "Why," Blystone asked the group, "would you be talking in January about a plan that you know you won't be happy with if you achieve it? That sounds like a pretty boring 12 months to me."

Blystone then turned his back to the division executives and asked them to raise their hands as he got to an EPS number that would make them proud, starting at 75 cents and going up in 25-cent increments. Chuck Bowman, director of financial analysis and head of SPX's EVA implementation, counted hands and told Blystone to stop when he reached $3 a share. Bowman translated the EPS number into EVA and parceled out dollar amounts of EVA stretch improvement targets to each of the divisions. The stretch goal came to $25 million, or nearly six times the $4.2 million of expected EVA improvement built into SPX's bonus plan that year. If the company met its stretch goal, it would achieve as much EVA improvement in one year as investors were expecting it to produce over the next five years. And, SPX managers would get bonuses five times as large as their target bonuses.

"People were extremely uncomfortable as they left the meeting," says Blystone. "That is part of the objective. Stretch is a mind-set that uses discomfort to stimulate thinking." A sense of discomfort is one of the common traits that Collins and Porras found at the visionary companies they examined in *Built to Last*. Discomfort—with where you are and with what you must achieve to remain on top—is one of the mechanisms those companies use to keep managers on a restless quest to constantly do better. Stretch provides ample discomfort. Says Blystone: "The whole idea of stretch is that you want people, as individuals and as a group, to do more than they, or you, can possibly understand how to achieve. Stretch goals are often considered impossible at the outset, but once you achieve the first one, it becomes the standard and then you go on to the next level."

Not that Blystone expects every manager to actually achieve the stretch goal each year. They are an aspiration, after all. But they also are real goals that he expects to be taken seriously. "We're not going to shoot a manager for doing all the right things and still not getting a stretch goal," he says. "What we're going to shoot you for is if you set too low a target and easily blow by it, or if you set a real tough target and then give up on it." Blystone sees this striving for the seemingly unattainable as an essential requirement for success. "To operate with a stretch mind-set means accepting that quantum change is not only possible, but absolutely necessary if you are going to remain competitive," he says. "Stretch is a way to stay out in front of change and lead rather than sitting back and reacting to change. We think staying ahead of change is critical to staying in business and creating value."

The SPX managers returned a month after that first meeting with detailed plans for achieving some, but far from all, of their stretch goals. Bowman designed a one-page document that separates planned EVA improvement into various components, including revenue growth, cost management, working capital management, profit margins, and the like. The objective is to add more planned improvements to the list each month until they add up to the stretch target. "Everyone had a problem with stretch the first year," says one manager. "It was unbelievable the way John [Blystone] drove it. He was always there asking, 'How are you getting to stretch? What have you done today?'"

Their shared discomfort with Blystone's unrelenting emphasis on stretch also had the effect of annealing the division managers into a genuine team, especially when it began to appear that they might actually achieve their audacious ambitions. The managers have to make monthly presentations to their peers about the specific actions they are taking to achieve the stretch EVA targets. "There is tremendous pressure on the division presidents to show that they are carrying their fair share," says Bowman. "The pressure is pride. They want their peers to know that they are moving the business forward." They also pitch in to help those who are faltering, mostly by sharing new ideas and practices that have worked well in their own operations. That didn't happen before.

To the amazement of everyone (except Blystone), SPX achieved the unachievable in 1996, generating $26.6 million of EVA improvement. That wiped out more than half the $51 million EVA deficit that SPX had in 1995. Based on the company's stock price when it adopted EVA, the market had expected that it would take SPX eight to 10 years to get EVA up to zero. Now it appeared that the company might achieve that milestone in just two or three years. The payoff for managers was enormous. The top five executives in the company's proxy had target bonuses that totaled $970,000 for 1996, but their earned bonuses came to 5.1 times that, or $4.8 million. Blystone alone earned a bonus of just over $2 million, versus a target of $397,159. He took home $947,296 of the total, with the balance going into the bonus bank.

Bonus multiples of more than five times target would seem to imply that the amount of expected EVA improvement built into the bonus plan was too low, and that SPX management had successfully sandbagged the board of directors. Not so. For one thing, keep in mind that the 1996 increase in EVA amounted to roughly 2.5% of sales. An increase of that magnitude in the after-tax rate of return on sales would be enormous at just about any mature manufacturer. More important, the standout performance of SPX stock makes it clear that the company did indeed perform far better than investors had expected. The stock nearly tripled over the course of the year, jumping from $15.375 in early January to $40.375 in late December, and was the 22nd-best-performing stock on the New York Stock Exchange that year. SPX managers got a huge payday, but so did shareholders. SPX's MVA jumped by $348 million in 1996, from minus $93 million to plus $255 million.

The SPX operating units achieved such stunning results by ferreting out every possible EVA improvement. Soon after Blystone arrived, for example, he learned that the capital budget for 1996 was $45 million. He pointed out to the division heads that depreciation charges amounted to only $30 million, and said he wanted capital spending held to that level or less. "Normally when you do that in turnaround situations, you get a lot of wailing and gnashing of teeth," says Blystone. "Well, because they were rolling out EVA at the same time and were looking at capital differently than they had before, people said, 'I guess I don't need that.' " Capital expenditures for the year came to $22 million, less than half originally planned.

One example of the new capital awareness involved a warehouse in Owatonna, Minnesota. SPX was closing another warehouse in Roseville, Michigan, and moving that inventory to Owatonna. The managers in Owatonna planned to accommodate the added inventory by building a new, $5-million warehouse. EVA analysis soon changed their minds. Instead of adding space, the division bought a $500,000 logistical software system that enabled it to speed deliveries to customers, reduce inventories, and forgo the added space. "Customers were happier, inventories went down, and the result was a tremendous EVA play," Blystone boasts.

SPX's Contech division, which makes die-cast aluminum and magnesium components for steering systems, became equally frugal. The division needed two new robots for its foundry. The cost was $2 million for the pair, and there was no way of economizing by doing without them or just buying one. "But they thought about how much it would affect their compensation because now they are thinking like owners," says Blystone. "Someone came up with the bright idea of buying two demonstration models, provided that the manufacturer would touch up the paint and provide the same warranty. The price was just $1 million for the two." Contech also achieved $959,000 of EVA improvement through better metals procurement. That was equal to the EVA Contech would have earned on an additional $15 million of sales.

EVA analysis sometimes showed that spending *more* money was the wiser course. Warren Simons, director of finance for SPX's Power Team, which makes high-pressure hydraulic tools, approved a plan to ship goods to an Australian warehouse by air freight instead of the surface transportation it had been using. The proposal calculated that added freight costs would come to $23,000 a year after taxes, but that the faster deliveries would enable the warehouse to reduce its goods on hand by $250,000, saving some $27,500 in capital charge. The EVA gain was only $4,500, but every bit counts. SPX had literally hundreds of similar small initiatives, many of them involving inventory controls or procurement, that added up to a sterling achievement. Its die-casting operation, for example, is so lean that its inventory turns approach 50 a year, and it routinely has negative working capital. Filtran, the transmission filter business, shipped 12 million parts in 1996 with zero defects.

Blystone gives a large share of the credit for SPX's performance to EVA, which he says works extremely well with stretch goals. "EVA makes it safer to strive hard for a goal," he says. "Because it takes both the balance sheet and the income statement into account, we have found that you can push very, very hard without breaking anything." The uncapped feature of the bonus plan also supports stretch goals by providing a constant and continuous incentive for better performance. "The thing I like about our compensation system is that you're not moving the goalposts in or out," he says. "They are what they are. If you get really aggressive, focused leaders, that's a game they love to play." Blystone adds that the bonus plan has been "a key competitive advantage in attracting the talent we need, and that is another way EVA supports stretch."

While division managers focused on the details in 1996, Blystone began to redraw the big picture. First, he completed the reorganization into two operating divisions: Service Solutions (which includes diagnostic and testing equipment, essential tools, and administration of dealer service programs for car makers) and Vehicle Components. He also sold off Sealed Power, the company's original piston-ring business, and Hy-Lift, a small operation that makes valve-train components for auto engines. He also got rid of a marina and restaurant that SPX had acquired along with a palatial headquarters building several years before. Selling Hy-Lift was a minor matter; selling the Sealed Power piston-ring business was a big deal.

SPX began life as The Piston Ring Company in 1911 and changed its name to Sealed Power in 1931; the company didn't take the name SPX until 1988. Sealed Power had a dominant share of the U.S. piston-ring market and a return on capital so high that the company will not say what it was. However, it was being pressed by auto companies to expand its production facilities overseas, and the prospective returns on the new investment didn't look nearly so promising. SPX was considering the international expansion when Dana Corporation, a much larger auto-parts company that also had a piston-ring division, offered it $233 million for Sealed Power in October 1996. It was an offer SPX couldn't refuse. The price was higher, though Blystone won't reveal how much higher, than the present value of the future EVA that Sealed Power was expected to generate under SPX's ownership.

The sale of Sealed Power also fit with Blystone's vision of SPX's future. The core business became specialty tools and the other automotive maintenance equipment that SPX sells to car dealers and service centers, but the company's view of that market is now radically different. Instead of focusing on the $5.7-billion market for specialty and general tools, SPX is now targeting the entire $350-billion vehicle service market. As Blystone sees it, SPX now gets only $1 of the

$500 per vehicle that owners spend on service each year, leaving $499 per vehicle as a broader window to view its true growth potential. What Blystone envisions is something he calls vehicle service solutions, which involves integrating state-of-the-art tools and equipment with service information and data that will improve the productivity and quality of vehicle servicing worldwide. He hopes to achieve this with systems that integrate the service process from work order through diagnosis and repair, to inventory tracking and reordering, and to customer invoicing and follow-up.

To that end, SPX formed a strategic alliance with the Hewlett Packard Company early in 1997 to jointly develop products that leverage HP's leadership in measurement, communications, and computers with SPX's expertise in vehicle diagnostics. SPX also formed a marketing alliance with Mac Tools, a division of Stanley Works that sells to aftermarket auto service centers, and obtained North American marketing rights to ALLDATA Corporation's automotive information. ALLDATA is the leading electronic publisher of automotive repair information. SPX also acquired AR Brasch, a publisher of technical manuals for vehicles, and organized an enterprise alliance of shop equipment manufacturers to develop a standard, plug-and-play interface for repair equipment and information.

The alliances with HP and Mac Tools reflect a new willingness, common among EVA companies, to team up with others or outsource rather than trying to capture all the revenues from a product or service area by going it alone. Says Bowman, referring to the agreement with Mac Tools: "Why should we own trucks when Mac Tools already has a fleet of them and knows how to operate them efficiently? Capital should be invested in the company that knows that part of the business best."

What about stretch targets in 1997? When the division heads came in for their meeting in January of that year, most of their operating plans translated into bonus multiples of two or less, versus the average of 5.1 for 1996. "Why the hell would you want to pay yourself less this year than you got paid last year?" Blystone asked the group.

At his prodding, the group agreed to a stretch target of $25 million of EVA improvement again that year. As it turned out, EVA improvement came in at $18.8 million, less than the stretch target but still quite commendable. It was sufficient to push the stock price from $40.375 in December 1996 to $70.125 in December 1997. By the end of the first quarter of 1998 the stock had been above $78 a share, or more than five times what it was when Blystone arrived just 27 months before. And SPX generated positive EVA in the first half of 1998, six years ahead of schedule. In a little over two years, Blystone was well on the way to transforming SPX from a prosaic toolmaker into a high-tech, information-based growth company.

Afterword

Becoming an EVA Company

G. Bennett Stewart III

At an EVA conference in Atlanta in May 1995, Geoffrey Colvin, the editorial director of *FORTUNE* magazine, presented a handsome trophy to Coca-Cola CEO Roberto Goizueta, saluting Coke for becoming the No. 1 wealth-creating company in the United States. "I can assure you," Goizueta said, "that we would not be the No. 1 market value added company today if we had not adopted EVA in the early 1980s. . . . Whenever I am asked how to do it, I always offer two short pieces of advice. First, make it simple. Second, make it accountable."

Many important refinements in the EVA program have occurred since Coke first came on board, but Goizueta's advice remains valid today. To implement EVA properly, keep it simple and keep it accountable. To make it simple, EVA must become the focal point for managing the business. Concentrating on EVA is what it takes to unite and clarify decision making. It is not enough to add EVA to everything else. EVA must *replace* everything else. Otherwise, EVA will not be simple, but will only make managing more complex. How can EVA become the focal point? To begin with, increasing EVA must be embraced as the company's main mission, and top management should make a forceful, public commitment to that goal. As Coke explained it in its 1993 annual report:

> [We have] a precise focus on why we exist: to create real value for our shareholders over the long term. We believe the total returns we generate for our shareholders are directly driven by the economic profit [EVA] that we create. We define economic profit as our net operating profit after taxes in excess of our overall cost of capital. Over the past 10 years, our economic profit has grown at an average annual rate of 27 percent.

Creating wealth is the end, and increasing EVA is the means. With such a pronouncement in its annual report, there is no mistaking that Coke's ultimate aim is to create shareholder wealth. It is not, as you might think, to sell more Coca-Cola products (although it obviously has to do that very well to create shareholder wealth). Is that a bold statement? Sure. Is it also a wise statement? Absolutely. For one thing, no one at Coke can suffer the delusion that his or her continued employment derives from anything other than sustaining a vital, wealth-creating enterprise. Trying hard and making good products are just not good enough. Coke sets a higher standard of excellence for its people, and they know it. But Coke has also been fair to them by stating what it takes to win, what is the definition of success, and how the score will be kept: to increase EVA as much as possible.

Many senior managers find it exceedingly difficult to own up to their responsibility and to express their unabashed yearning to create shareholder wealth. Contrast Coke's unambiguous commitment with this squishy comment from former Hewlett Packard CEO John Young as reported in *Built to Last* (an otherwise excellent book offering many suggestions complementary to EVA, such as the adoption of bold stretch targets):

> Maximizing shareholder wealth has always been way down the list [of our priorities]. Yes, profit is a cornerstone of what we do—it is a measure of our contribution and a means of self-financed growth—but it

> has never been the point in and of itself. The point, in fact, is to win, and winning is judged in the eye of the customer and by doing something you can be proud of. There is a symmetry of logic in this. If we provide real satisfaction to real customers—we will be profitable.

If only it were so. A counter example demonstrates it is not. In 1997, GM had worldwide revenues of $178 billion, the most of any company in the world. Since people do not operate against their self-interest, we can safely assume that GM's customers were getting real satisfaction from buying GM cars and trucks. Taking John Young's definition of winning at face value, GM must be the best company around and revenues are the measure of success. But Young surely does not believe that, and even GM's own managers would have to concede that the company's performance has been disappointing. They simply have not been able to provide their customers with satisfaction at a price that enables the firm to cover all of its operating and capital costs, and that has hurt the stock price considerably. But in so doing GM has hardly been alone. Many large Far Eastern conglomerates have seen their stock prices plunge as a preoccupation with gaining market share and enhancing customer satisfaction lulled them into spending capital as if it was free.

As Hewlett Packard has undeniably been a successful company, the views of its top management should be taken seriously. But it is important to realize that HP has for many years used a backdoor version of EVA. At HP, the cost of capital enters through a unique financing strategy and the way that strategy has been communicated to employees. HP has long relied on retained earnings to fund growth. With rare exceptions, HP eschews debt and refuses to issue new equity. That policy mathematically limits HP's sustainable growth rate—that is, what can be achieved by internally generated funds—to the product of its earnings retention rate and the rate of return it earns on its capital. For example, if the board voted to pay out 25% of earnings as a dividend, then for HP to grow at a 15% rate it would need to earn a 20% return on its investments, after taxes (20% return multiplied by 75% retained equals a 15% growth rate).

By telling its managers that generating profit was necessary as a source of cash to fuel growth, HP convinced them, in effect, that capital has a cost that must be earned, and that profit was essential. That contrivance set up an implicit hurdle rate that those managers knew they had to beat when using retained capital, and it made HP into a profitable company when measured by EVA. But that essential message was conveyed in a roundabout way and was not amplified through performance measures, decision procedures, or incentive programs. No one can say for sure, but it is quite likely HP would have been even more successful if its management had welcomed EVA with open arms through the front door instead of allowing EVA to sneak in through the back.

Yes, Mr. Young, the point is to win. But what is winning? Profits do not automatically flow from satisfying customers as you suggest; only revenues do. The only intellectually honest answer is that winning is creating shareholder wealth for the simple reason that the shareholders are paid last, after all other factors of production have been paid. And that, in turn, takes producing as much EVA as possible. Why not say that, loud and clear? How can the man in the street be expected to embrace capitalism and free markets if the titans of industry either do not understand or are afraid to admit that building wealth is the ultimate aim of the business organization?

Making EVA simple in the manner that Goizueta suggests requires more than expressing a resolute commitment. It takes action. It takes weaving EVA so firmly into the fabric of the company's planning and managing processes that EVA is easy, inescapable, and irreversible. Plants, products, and business lines should be measured and evaluated directly in terms of the contribution each makes to corporate EVA. A company should not measure its EVA once a year after the year has gone by, as EVA groupies do, but month by month. EVA should not be a supplement to the reporting process, a line on the page, or one measure in a "balanced scorecard." EVA must be the bedrock upon which the entire reporting process is built.

In a typical EVA company the first page of the monthly report is the EVA summary. It presents a simplified calculation of EVA—sales less operating costs less capital costs—but with the ability to "drill down" to details at the click of a mouse or turn of a page. EVA and its components are compared against budget and the prior year's results, with significant variances flagged. Typically, the second page is the diagnostic report called "EVA Drivers." That is where other measures are linked together in a cause-and-effect chain that explains movements in EVA. This "integrated scorecard" is arrayed as a pyramid, with EVA at the apex. At the base are a concise group of key operating measures, the things field people relate to and can directly control. Those operating signals are tied to the outcomes for a select set of financial measures that in turn account directly for movements in EVA.

The EVA Drivers report can be organized by function, by market, or, better, by process. However organized, it is useful for diagnosing and benchmarking performance, for enabling managers to visualize and control trade-offs, and for communicating to everyone the role they have to play in increasing EVA. Most important, it is a constant reminder that increasing EVA is the main goal and that other outcomes and measures are interesting and useful only as means to achieving that end.

EVA must also help shape plans, projects, and budgets. Because the present value of EVA determines shareholder wealth, new initiatives should be pursued only if they are likely to increase the stream of EVAs that the company will generate in the future. This rule should be applied not only to formal capital projects, but to all decisions, even those occurring on the literal or figurative shop floor. EVA should reach beyond operations to engage staff departments as well. Financial strategies, for instance, should be selected to minimize the cost of capital. And there is still one more thing top management must do to make EVA simple: It must use EVA as the cornerstone in communications with the board of directors and with the research analysts and money managers who increasingly are interested in recommending or buying the stocks of EVA companies.

The second ingredient for a successful EVA implementation is accountability, which can best be achieved by paying managers for increasing EVA via the special bonus plan outlined in Chapter 7. Only then will managers think and act like owners because they are paid like owners. Only then will they have the incentive to use the EVA reporting, planning, and capital budgeting machinery instead of working around it. Only then can top management feel comfortable delegating greater decision making authority and raising capital spending thresholds.

The bonus derived from EVA should be displayed as the third page in the monthly report. With that in hand, managers see the pot of gold accumulating in their bonus accrual account each month as the year unfolds, or contrariwise, see how deep a hole they are digging for themselves. There is nothing like that constant tangible reminder of success and failure to get a manager's juices flowing. The bonus calculation should also be embedded into the capital budgeting and decision making templates that project and discount EVA. No longer will managers consider a sensitivity analysis to be a perfunctory, theoretical exercise they care little about. Now they will be keenly interested in how the project might affect their personal risk/return profile. That connection to their bonus, and not some ratcheting up of the cost of capital, is the only real way to get managers motivated to manage risk. The point, in sum, is to inextricably stitch together performance measurement, decision making, and incentive compensation via EVA. Nothing could be simpler or more powerful.

With these basic precepts in mind, a good way to appreciate how to become an EVA company is to walk through the program employed by a recent adopter, Federal-Mogul Corporation. When the wheels of its implementation first began turning in the second quarter of 1997, Federal-Mogul was a $2-billion auto parts manufacturer and distributor with a share price of $28. Within one year of setting

EVA in motion, the Detroit-based company had managed to more than double both its sales and its stock price. After a stunning string of acquisitions, sales for 1998 were running at more than $5 billion and the stock price had rocketed to nearly $70 a share. Federal-Mogul provides a classic example of how to implement EVA quickly and decisively in the face of overwhelming change and challenge. It also illustrates how the stock market is increasingly anticipating the benefits of EVA before they materialize.

Under prior management Federal-Mogul had unwisely integrated forward into the retail distribution of auto parts. Seduced by the higher margins and stock price multiples accorded established retail chains such as Autozone and Pep Boys, beginning in 1990 Federal-Mogul built an extensive chain of retail outlets throughout Europe, Latin America, Africa, and Australia. This represented a massive bet on a business arena far afield from Federal-Mogul's core strength of making well-engineered parts for the original equipment manufacturers (OEMs). While at first delivering impressive sales and earnings gains, the integration move ultimately failed to produce a higher stock price. The strategy failed because it led to inadequate returns and negative EVAs, although those measures were not on the company's radar screen at the time. Federal-Mogul's share price reached a peak value of almost $40 a share in 1993, but with its EVA plunging in 1996 to a deficit of about $120 million, the stock crashed to $16 by the third quarter of that year.

Fearing for the company's survival, the board replaced the CEO with one of its own, Steve Miller, a turnaround specialist who had been instrumental in saving Chrysler years before. He quickly recruited Richard Snell, the head of Tenneco Automotive, to succeed him. Taking the helm in November 1996, Snell wasted little time in making decisive changes. Within three months, he announced the disposal of the struggling retail business, and he hired Thomas Ryan, his chief financial officer and right-hand man at Tenneco Automotive, appointing him Federal-Mogul's new CFO. Impressed with the new leaders and the restructuring moves, investors boosted the share price from $16 to $28 by the end of April 1997, a 75% gain in value even before EVA had arrived on the scene. Snell and Ryan both wanted to seize upon EVA as an important element in their turnaround and growth strategy for Federal-Mogul. Several factors motivated them. For one, they were familiar with EVA through their experience with Tenneco's homegrown version. They liked the elegance of EVA as a measure and were convinced it reliably linked to stock market performance. But they also wanted to include the special EVA bonus plan and decision making applications that had not been part of the Tenneco program.

The new executives also felt EVA could help to restore morale and refocus management. The prior CEO had been preoccupied with generating a neat progression in earnings per share. He put field managers under intense pressure to do things they felt made no sense, things that they knew would hurt the business, just to reach the near-term earnings targets he was convinced the stock market wanted. Equally discouraging, middle managers found most decisions directed from the top down to achieve grand strategic goals. Their ability to contribute by leading continuous improvement initiatives emanating from the bottom up was given short shrift.

The new management team reached its final decision to adopt EVA in May and, following the Goizueta dictum, was quick to declare its commitment. A press release on May 22, 1997, stated that "Stern Stewart, the company which is focusing America's corporate leaders on economic value added (EVA) as the best indicator of success, has been engaged to assist in the implementation of their EVA framework at Federal-Mogul. . . . Economic Value Added will be a way of life for all of our team members at Federal-Mogul. We are committed to creating value for our shareholders. EVA has the strongest correlation of any financial measure to a company's stock price. We will be driven by and measured by the wealth created for our shareholders."

There can be no better way to begin an EVA implementation. A statement like that one tells everyone the CEO and executive team are on board. Questions shift from if and whether to how and how soon. Another reason is to boost the stock price. Considering that many stock analysts and investors are aware of the benefits of EVA, it should not be surprising that Federal-Mogul's share price rose nearly 4%, from about $28 to $29, as the EVA commitment was first announced, and was up to $35 a little more than a month later.

The EVA implementation was slated to unfold over a 10-month period from June 1997 through April 1998, and was charted to instill all four main EVA applications through three overlapping phases. As a mnemonic device, the main applications are described by words beginning with the letter *m*. The first two, to develop and institute EVA as a *measure* and as a *management system*, are fused into one phase. The second phase, using EVA for *motivation*, is concerned with tailoring the special incentive plans that make managers into owners. The third phase firmly implants EVA as a *mind-set* with important constituencies inside and outside of the firm. In other words, it covers training and communications. Federal-Mogul formed a senior steering committee consisting of Snell and Ryan, plus Alan Johnson, the chief operating officer; Dick Randazzo, the head of human resources; and Chuck Grant, head of corporate development. The senior committee contributed by expressing support, and by meeting every four to six weeks to review progress and provide counsel. Snell put Dick Randazzo in charge to send the message that EVA was intended to change behavior and was not principally a finance initiative. He formed an implementation team to carry out the project. Consisting of about 10 people drawn from a cross section of staff areas and supplemented by a cadre of up-and-coming line managers, the team was spearheaded full-time by Jeff Kaminski, a former managing director of the company's Australian subsidiary.

The implementation advanced down several tracks at once. One was to provide the company team with a first-pass look at EVA profit estimates for Federal-Mogul, its units and its peers, and the relation of EVA to stock prices and MVA. A second track took the team into the field to meet operating people. Those meetings convinced line people that the head office would not simply impose the EVA program on them without seeking their input. They liked the idea that they could help to shape the EVA program to be consistent with behavior that they felt it was important to promote or preserve. For instance, some managers initially expressed the concern that EVA would stifle growth or that it was only about cutting costs, but they came away convinced that would be far from the truth.

The EVA team also wanted to defuse other misperceptions. Federal-Mogul people were fearful that EVA would be used to rank and summarily discharge managers of negative or bottom-of-the-barrel units before they had a chance to improve. There were palpable sighs of relief when they learned the program was not intended to lay blame for mistakes made under a prior regime, and that EVA was an opportunity to wipe the slate clean and start fresh. It was explained that producing an increase in EVA was what mattered, not its current level, and that people would be furnished with the time, training, tools, and incentives to help them carry out the turnaround they all knew was necessary. Almost from the start a ubiquitous enthusiasm for the program welled up and the willingness of field people to contribute their insights was high.

During these meetings the team also gathered undiluted, first-hand impressions about financial management practices and incentive plans to help them tailor the EVA program to fit Federal-Mogul. As is typical of most firms, they found bad procedures forcing good people to adopt patterns of suboptimal behavior. Depending on the firm, those can involve deficiencies in cost accounting and transfer pricing, compensation arrangements and performance metrics, capital spending thresholds and hurdle rates, business and financial literacy, and, in what turned out to be a particularly significant issue for Federal-Mogul, the organizational structure. Almost impossible to perceive from the distant remove of the head office, the subtle and intertwined failings of existing management practices are invariably addressed as part of the EVA program and cannot logically be separated from it. Identifying and cataloging the problems constituted an essential first step.

No implementation can commence in earnest until an optimal structure of EVA centers has been determined. EVA centers are units and subunits for which EVA will be measured and managed on an ongoing basis. The consolidated company is the ultimate EVA center, and the aim is to increase EVA at that level as much as possible. But separating a company into cascading layers of EVA centers improves the line of sight of its managers and forges a closer link between decision and outcome and between pay and performance.

But as with everything in life, diminishing returns and countervailing costs offset and eventually overwhelm the benefits of greater segmentation. More than the additional data tracking expenses, the most significant drawback is that uncooperative behavior may set in as each individual center attempts to maximize its EVA at the expense of companywide performance. Tying the incentives of local managers to aggregate financial or stock performance can mitigate this tunnel vision, as can the development of transfer prices that properly allocate the costs and benefits of decisions among the affected EVA centers. However, none of those remedies is without expense or entirely effective, so at some point the separation of a company into smaller and smaller centers becomes counterproductive.

The designation of the EVA centers was even more pressing than usual for Federal-Mogul. The top management team had sensed, and their middle managers confirmed, that the company's organizational structure had to be rethought. The main problem was that Federal-Mogul had been split into two divisions that did not work well together. All manufacturing activities along with the sales of OEM products were tracked in one unit, while the sales and distribution (but not the manufacturing) of aftermarket products were contained in a second unit. Though producing all the products, the manufacturing plants were credited with the profit on only the sales of OEM products and were reimbursed for just the estimated cost of producing the aftermarket products.

This arrangement discouraged manufacturing and aftermarket managers from cooperating. The tension was heightened by the aftermarket division frequently issuing special orders for small lots with urgent due dates. The cost-based reimbursement that manufacturing received from the aftermarket division was probably below its real cost of servicing such taxing demands. The plant managers also quickly realized that the established transfer price had not been designed to compensate them for the cost of the capital tied up to make aftermarket products. Once EVA was adopted, servicing aftermarket sales would shift from a near breakeven contribution to accounting profit to a sizable EVA drag. As far as the plant managers were concerned, a change in organization or transfer price, or both, was essential before they could support the EVA program.

After testing several formulations, Dick Randazzo and the EVA team recommended combining aftermarket and OEM profit and also consolidating the profit way above the level of the plants and geographic regions. Top management agreed, having known instinctively that a bigger, more coherent picture was needed. The principal EVA centers would become three global systems groups, each representing the worldwide manufacturing and sales of a related cluster of products distributed through both the OEM and aftermarket channels. Aftermarket was to remain a separate, fourth EVA center; but, in order to provide an incentive for teamwork, its profit was to be counted twice—once in the three global systems groups, where all manufacturing occurred, and again in the aftermarket group itself.

The individual product lines and plants might eventually become subsidiary EVA centers in their own right, providing ancillary information for decision making and eventually a basis for more decentralized bonus plans. A decision about that would be deferred until more detailed accounting information could be tracked. From a pure accounting point of view, measuring product- and plant-level EVA appears to be a trivial exercise. But to do it right, to measure EVA in a way that encourages continuous improvement and teamwork between interfacing units such as manufacturing and marketing, is actually one of the most intellectually challenging questions in the economics of the firm. Most companies get the interfaces terribly wrong, and that is why they burn up a considerable portion of their store of human capital in organizational friction.

One reason is that cost accounting dogma creates perverse incentives for manufacturing and other internal sourcing centers. Such units are typically allowed to recover only their costs (and usually only operating costs at that) through the charges they pass on to downstream revenue-generating units, and at best to break even. As with the traditional public utility, there is little incentive for them to aggressively pursue efficiencies, because any cost reductions they achieve are simply passed to downstream entities without comment or congratulations. But by establishing a formula for sharing efficiency gains, new transfer pricing methods are becoming available to rescue internal sourcing units from the purgatory of cost recovery treatment and transform them into legitimate EVA centers.

At last possessing a logical organizational skeleton on which to graft the EVA system, the team next turned to selecting an optimal way to measure EVA. The steering committee stipulated that the EVA definition should reflect the economics of decisions with reasonable accuracy while still being relatively easy to explain and administer, and that it should require no more than 12 rules to transform raw accounting numbers into a more accurate estimate of EVA. The team considered 25 potential adjustments but decided to implement only 10. A discussion of a few will demonstrate that encouraging managers to behave in the interest of the shareholders, and not achieving theoretical precision, is always the aim in defining EVA.

The team first considered how best to isolate operating from financing decisions. They discussed the appropriate EVA treatment for seasonal financing and lease commitments, early payment discounts and pension funding policies, purchase versus pooling acquisitions, securitized receivables and excess cash, and so forth. CFO Tom Ryan was particularly eager to get field managers to send the cash they earned to the head office faster. As happens in many companies, local country managers had a habit of running unauthorized interest-rate or currency speculation casinos alongside their legitimate operating businesses. Wanting to shut down those worrisome sideline businesses, Ryan insisted that the EVA definition strongly encourage a swift repatriation of excess cash. The remedy was relatively straightforward, if not severe. Excess cash was to be included in the capital base subject to the capital charge, but the related investment income was to be excluded from NOPAT, a treatment that makes it exceedingly expensive to hoard cash. This applies only to the individual EVA centers, of course, and is eliminated upon consolidation. As with transfer prices, such an adjustment is invisible to the world at large and yet can be extremely important in molding behavior inside a company.

The team also wanted to encourage managers to reduce the company's tax bill and to factor tax considerations into decisions. They decided that each EVA center should be charged for the cash taxes due on its operating profit, and not for the accounting tax provision. But rather than estimating that tax bill by country or entity, which is an accurate though time-consuming approach that some EVA companies choose, Federal-Mogul opted for a simpler method. The company would charge each unit for tax by applying a rolling average of the corporatewide cash tax rate on operating income over the past several years. That gave an incentive to minimize taxes but smoothed away distractions of yearly swings and discontinuities.

Three more refinements to the EVA definition are noteworthy. The first was to add restructuring charges to the balance sheet instead of expensing them, treating the losses as investments on which management would have to produce a minimum return. By doing so, Federal-Mogul would be better able to clean house and to restructure companies it acquired because its managers could be rewarded, or at least not penalized, in the short term for making the right long-term decision.

A second set of refinements covered acquisitions. Among other things, the goodwill amortization arising from purchase acquisitions would be added back both to earnings and to the capital on the balance sheet, a conversion to cash flow accounting that would have managers asking the right question. Can we generate enough cash from the target to cover the cost of the capital we have expended to buy it? While the EVA team did not know it at the time, that seemingly innocuous adjustment was soon to play a vital role in supporting top management's growth strategy.

The third adjustment stemmed directly from discussions with field managers. They expressed widespread agreement that the firm's research and development outlays should be capitalized for EVA purposes and written off over time instead of charged to earnings right away as standard accounting requires. They felt that technological excellence in design and manufacturing was the firm's core competency, and yet spending in those areas had been unduly constrained, particularly in the fourth quarter, due to prior management's earnings addiction. They felt it would be sending exactly the wrong signal if capitalization treatment were not adopted.

The one exception to the distasteful research experience occurred in Germany where the country manager, Willhelm Schmelzer, had worked around the disruptive earnings constraint. Over a period of seven years he squirreled away money in accounting reserves so he could secretly fund research to develop a new, high-strength bearing that has become the industry standard. "Before, I had to hide what I was doing in order to do what was right for the company," says Schmelzer. "Now, with EVA, we can do what is right and feel good about it. My people and I are really charged up about this." Schmelzer has finally gotten the recognition he deserves: Snell put him in charge of one of the three global systems groups.

A special study was undertaken to determine the life of Federal-Mogul's research spending. The variation in shareholder wealth that could be explained by a simple regression with EVA was raised from 33% to almost 50% by assuming R&D was written off over five years instead of all at once. After considering the company's own product development experiences and divining management intuition, it was agreed that Federal-Mogul would treat research as a five-year asset for EVA measurement purposes. With that, the managers could feel freer to invest for the long term, and yet shareholders also would be assured that managers would feel accountable for getting results.

As the work team was constructing the scaffolding of the EVA program, Federal-Mogul's top executives were nailing down a bold strategy, providing another example of how EVA and stretch goals go together. In July 1997 Snell gathered the company's top 150 leaders and asked them to commit to ambitious goals. On September 2 he revealed management's stretch plan to the *Wall Street Journal.* Incredibly, Federal-Mogul expected to quintuple revenues—to $10 billion—by 2002. The company also targeted a zero defect rate and aimed to generate positive EVA, something it had not done for the past seven years, in order "to show that the company intends to become profitable, and not just boost sales." Snell emphasized the sales goal could not be achieved without acquisitions.

Finding the strategy much to their liking, Salomon Brothers analyst Jack Kiernan and his auto research team initiated coverage of Federal-Mogul. In a report released September 23, they based a strong buy recommendation in part on benefits expected from the EVA program:

> Management has a strong acquisition track record, and the developing EVA discipline could enhance it. . . . We believe a principal reason why Stern Stewart is at Federal-Mogul is to institute a compensation plan based upon EVA. As managers begin to understand how much EVA is expected from them, and then aim to beat it, we anticipate that improvements in EVA could be dramatic. That, in our opinion, is a hidden catalyst for the stock.

On September 25, a little more than three weeks after his *Wall Street Journal* interview, Snell announced a $2-billion bid for T&N, a British auto parts company with $2.7 billion in sales that ranked near the bottom of Stern Stewart's MVA ranking of United Kingdom firms. Federal-Mogul's stock rose $3.75 to close the day at $37.25 a share. Within a week Federal-Mogul had sealed the deal by raising its bid from $2 billion to $2.4 billion. With the news that T&N had capitulated, thereby paving the way for the formation of the world's largest supplier of engine systems, Federal-Mogul's stock rose an additional $3.75 in one day, closing at $45. Following the EVA principle that debt within limits is cheaper than equity, and that the stock market ignores goodwill amortization and concentrates on cash flow, the deal was structured to be an all-cash transaction subject to the purchase accounting treatment.

The business logic of the deal was impeccable and the execution of the strategy flawless. Federal-Mogul was well on its way to achieving its audacious $10-billion sales goal, its stock price was significantly higher, and the train of events suggests that EVA had played a role, too. Even though by no means fully implemented, EVA had given the market confidence that management would not overpay and confidence that management would have a strong incentive to succeed in the aftermath. Investors also expected that Federal-Mogul would deploy EVA at T&N (as it has), and believed that that conversion could help to merge the cultures and hasten the turnaround of the target company.

Not content to rest on its laurels, Federal-Mogul announced on January 12, 1998, the acquisition of Fel Pro, another high-quality auto parts company with sales of about $500 million. Delighted at last to be on a winning team, Federal-Mogul middle managers began to circulate e-mails featuring a mock, two-inch-high headline reading, "Federal-Mogul tenders for the U.S. Government." It is safe to say that the company's managers are no longer demoralized.

Federal-Mogul was so committed to EVA that its implementation program continued unabated amid those intense acquisition and restructuring actions. A series of "expert training" programs was conducted in September 1997. Each company location had to send at least one person (usually the controller or a business planner) who would be responsible for helping the line people to use EVA for performance analysis and decision making. Some 100 experts were groomed in a series of intensive four-day training programs. They progressed from novice to black belt, eventually performing advanced modeling applications. For instance, they entered financial data for their own units into an EVA analysis software called FINANSEER®, and worked in teams to interpret the results and benchmark against peer companies.

The peak learning experience was matching wits with an EVA simulation game called Nightingale Brewers. In that full-day exercise, the players formed teams to run a hypothetical beer company for five years. Their mission: figure out how to increase its EVA as much as possible. They had to answer questions about adding and dropping capacity and product lines, outsourcing, distribution and purchasing strategies, automating, advertising, and more. Fun and competitive to play, the game helped the managers to understand how EVA could be used to manage day-to-day and long-range issues. It showed them why getting rid of a negative EVA investment is not always a good decision, and why cost cutting and shrinking is not the way to win in the long run. It showed the interrelated nature of many decisions, and that helped to foster teamwork. And it showed them how sound business judgment must always supplement a straightforward EVA analysis.

Conducted in the fourth month of the implementation, the expert training sessions signaled the beginning of the attack on the second of the four *m*'s, the EVA management system. Now was the time for the in-house experts to repay their education. They were each asked to submit some decision or capital budgeting project that they had successfully modeled and resolved using EVA. Touching upon a wide range of subjects, such as investing in new technology, responding to competitive threats, longer versus shorter production runs, pricing and credit terms, and many more, the best of those studies were honed into formal cases to be used later in broad-based management training.

Capital budgeting and planning templates were also updated and reworked to incorporate EVA. The company's "Appropriations Request Manual" was plagued with an unhealthy emphasis on internal rate of return as opposed to NPV, and it did not include a modern risk analysis method. It simply dictated using three different hurdle rates—15%, 20%, and 25%, after taxes—for varying circumstances where they were not really appropriate. Custom spreadsheets were prepared to facilitate decision making by considering the impact on projected EVA and by incorporating multiscenario simulation methods to analyze risk, a better procedure than asking managers to rely on more or less arbitrary costs of capital as a deciding factor. With more effective risk modeling coming on line, and anticipating that the EVA bonus plan would significantly increase the managers' exposure to risk, the steering committee agreed to mandate that a single, dollar-based cost of capital would apply to all operations worldwide, a significant and sensible simplification.

Other important policy changes also stemmed from the capital budgeting discussions. Top management abandoned the longstanding practice of rationing capital and raised the spending authority delegated to field managers. In the past, managers had wanted to get their hands on as much funding as possible to help them fuel growth in earnings per share. As a result, the head office set an overall limit on investment spending in an attempt to contain their voracious appetite for capital. That only made matters worse. It simply added incentive for field managers to overstate payoffs from their projects out of fear other managers were inflating theirs even more. Anticipating that EVA would cool the rabid desire for capital by making it costly, the steering committee relaxed the artificial constraints that prior administrations had invoked. They thought this seminal change in policy would signal their willingness to trust their managers and their desire to encourage more profitable growth. The effect was immediate. Middle managers pulled superfluous investment proposals off the table right away.

The pursuit of the third *m* of EVA, motivation, was launched as the project first began. Right from the start, the basic characteristics and design parameters of EVA bonus plans and equity alternatives were avidly discussed, and the perceived shortcomings in the existing incentive programs were flagged. After comparatively few conversations and simulations, top management committed to putting all key managers on EVA bonus plans for 1998 and extending EVA bonuses to all salaried employees as soon as possible. Human resources chief Randazzo was also quick to conclude that bonuses should be funded exclusively by EVA, a recommendation readily accepted by top management. Even though they had adopted ambitious goals for sales and quality, the executive team correctly wanted those to be viewed as means to the end of producing more EVA. They did reserve the right to modify slightly the overall size of the bonus pools that were funded by EVA in order to emphasize some other overarching qualitative theme, such as diversity. For managers farther down the chain of command, moreover, they permitted the EVA bonus pools to be paid out in part according to how well they had performed on other measures deemed to be direct EVA drivers, such as defect rates. But the fundamental principle of "no EVA improvement means no bonus" was to be preserved up and down the line.

In particular, the bonus for the top 55 executives was based solely on a strict formula for sharing the improvement in EVA according to the special incentive structure outlined in Chapter 7. The improvement would initially be measured relative to the EVA implied by the budget (too much change was occurring to use any other benchmark for 1998). In subsequent years, the improvement would be measured against EVA targets reset by simple formulas. Those formulas will build off the prior year's EVA but will also add multiyear EVA improvement targets that have been objectively calculated in advance to provide investors with an appropriate rate of return.

For 1998, about 350 of Federal-Mogul's managers and functional specialists will earn bonuses tied to EVA. Each person's bonus depends on some combination of the EVA produced by the four principal EVA centers and the consolidated company. As additional information becomes available, the intent is to forge an even closer bonus link to the contributions made by the individual plant managers and sales and marketing people. Opportunities to take EVA incentives to even lower levels, possibly to the shop floor as Herman Miller and SPX have done, will also be explored as time goes by. More than these details, the important point to grasp is that even in their first year and in the midst of a substantial reorganization of the company, the EVA bonus plans will succeed at Federal-Mogul.

The confidence that top management has secured in just a short time takes us to the realm of the fourth and most important *m* of EVA, mind-set. That is ultimately what drives the change in behavior and builds a winning team. Ideally, the mind-set indoctrination starts at the top and right up front, as it did with Federal-Mogul. Of course, not every CEO is so convinced or so passionate right away. In more conservative hands the commitment to EVA grows only as the CEO gains more familiarity with it, and that's fine, too. After the CEO, the top management team must cross the Rubicon (although in practice it is not uncommon for the order to be reversed). Right at the outset they should be provided with a presentation outlining the applications and benefits of EVA so they can be convinced on its merits. On rare occasions, an entire "familiarization study" is required just to construct the case that will persuade the senior team to give EVA the nod. For Federal-Mogul, that wasn't necessary. As Snell and Ryan had hoped, a three-hour presentation about EVA in April 1997 was enough to get the management team fired up. By the seventh month of the program, in December 1997, the top 20 executives were ready for a more thorough immersion. They had already gained a good feel for EVA and how it worked, but they were eager for meaty, challenging cases to cement their understanding of how to use EVA to drive operating and strategic decisions. Understandably, they were most keenly interested to learn how the EVA bonus plan would function in the coming year.

Once the senior team has been engaged, it is a good idea to develop a brochure to explain EVA fundamentals to the entire employee base. To do that, delegates from Federal-Mogul's investor relations and internal communications departments distributed a special EVA edition of the Federal-Mogul *World* newsletter. The oversized, four-page handout was a colorful but convincing document covering such topics as:

- What is EVA and how is it calculated?
- EVA as a management tool
- Three ways to improve EVA
- What EVA means to Federal-Mogul
- What can I do to increase EVA?
- Shareholder value and EVA
- What's been happening and what's next?
- Federal-Mogul embraces EVA as a way of life.

Carrying EVA incentives and training right to the shop floor is always possible, but for the initial implementation the EVA mind-set is usually implanted only as deep as the corps of middle managers and key functional specialists. That is the group most in need of practical, hands-on training. In the early months of 1998, as the project drew to a close, the implementation team synthesized and distilled the company's entire EVA program into a one-and-a-half-day workshop that is intended to reach many hundreds of those people.

As with everything else, Federal-Mogul took an unusually aggressive approach to cementing the support of its directors, and with good reason. The board is the body formally charged with corporate governance, and EVA can help it to reform governance from within, making heavy-handed interventions from external parties unlikely. At its July 1997 meeting, the entire complement of Federal-Mogul directors was provided with a succinct verbal primer about the EVA framework. Even in the tempestuous month of September, the board made time for a progress report. By December, they had heard enough. The EVA bonus plan was unanimously approved on the first vote.

This was also the first time a CEO had arranged a full-day EVA education program for his board. In February 1998 Snell and his fellow directors (excepting Steve Miller, who was busy rescuing Waste Management) attended an EVA workshop. After enduring EVA basic training in the morning, the board broke into two teams to take on the perilous and humbling Nightingale Brewers game in the afternoon. The results of that test match will not be revealed in this book.

A public company also needs to inform investors about its EVA program. From the start, Snell was quick to disclose his intention to move Federal-Mogul onto EVA and to announce EVA as a critical goal. Once the board formally approved the bonus in December, he wasted no time getting a more complete message out. On January 6, 1998, Snell and his executive team met with a large group of securities analysts in New York. They devoted considerable time to a discussion of the EVA definition, bonus plan, and goals, the use of EVA in decision making and training, and plans to integrate EVA into T&N. Many analysts requested more information, and Snell made sure they got it. He arranged a one-day workshop for 25 of them in February. Here are what two of them had to say:

> The explanation of the implementation and the EVA measure employed at FMO [Federal-Mogul] was very helpful. It is important for analysts to know how changes in the management of the income statement and balance sheet will affect EVA. . . . The excessive focus on EPS is wrong. It is clearly not how long-term value is created. . . . Compensation needs to be tied to returns, but this is difficult to do—EVA accomplishes this in a new and creative way. . . . I wish all the companies I invested in adopted EVA.
>
> Elizabeth M. Lilly, CFA
> Managing Partner
> Woodland Partners

Woodland Partners is among the largest holders of stock in both Federal-Mogul and SPX.

> The Nightingale Brewers EVA game was an excellent experience—it illustrated real-life decision making using EVA to make investments. . . . FMO's adoption of EVA is terrific—it is clear that top management is aligned with shareholders. . . . The key to make EVA work is top management really believing in it and living it as they have at FMO. . . . A misconception is that companies on EVA do not spend capital. At FMO it is the opposite, as they have decided that managers can spend as much as they want, but will be rewarded only if the projects create value.
>
> Eric Goldstein
> Associate Director
> Bear Stearns

On April 23, 1998, top executives met again with securities analysts. They discussed the integration of the acquired companies, reviewing expected synergies, but also revealed for the first time corresponding charges of over $1 billion. Asked by the analysts when they could next afford to finance a major acquisition, CEO Snell responded, "Right now," and revealed two bold moves designed to reload the growth cannon and enhance financial flexibility. Federal-Mogul would raise between $400 and $600 million in a public common stock offering in June, and the dividend would be slashed from 48 cents to just a penny a share.

Unveil a major restructuring charge, announce the overhang of a major new equity offering, and tell the world you are cutting the dividend to the bone, and what do you get? Traditional financial advisers would call for the undertaker, but they would be wrong, because an EVA company can break all the rules and still be rewarded. On the day after the analyst briefing, Federal-Mogul's stock price surged $6 a share to reach $65, representing a total gain of about 125% from the time the EVA implementation had commenced the year before. CEO Dick Snell tallies the experience with EVA thus far:

> When I arrived at Federal-Mogul I learned we had to struggle to address daunting business issues without the luxury of time. It could easily have taken years to tackle all our problems had they been addressed sequentially. EVA accelerated our ability to divest assets and focus on our manufacturing core, to restore earnings improvements, and to begin to grow by acquisition. EVA was the criterion we used to evaluate each and every action—whether for rationalization, continuous improvement, or growth. With the clarity it provided, EVA allowed us to complete our evaluations quickly and move on to the next challenge. We are confident that EVA will continue to help all of us to make better business decisions, to build a world-class company, and to enhance shareholder wealth.

As this case makes clear, instilling a wealth-building culture by adopting EVA is a considerable undertaking, and many senior executives are too intimidated even to begin the journey. But those leaders should realize that in today's hypercompetitive economy the riskiest strategy of all is not making the changeover, particularly if competitors are making the move. They should be emboldened also by knowing that nearly 300 companies have already succeeded in completing the EVA odyssey, and most of them, like Federal-Mogul, have benefited handily. But it is not an exaggeration to suggest that the most encouraging evidence is coming from the experiences of former communist countries that converted to free markets. The trek they made from totalitarianism to capitalism is as Everest to anthills more daunting than merely changing the culture of a company, no matter how large and complex it may be.

The strong case for bold governance reform first appeared in a comprehensive World Bank study of the 26 economies that had thrown off the shackles of communism. According to research published in June 1996, speedy reformers such as Poland and the Czech Republic suffered smaller falls in output and returned to growth more quickly than the slow movers. What worked best was "shock therapy" and what worked worst was "the Mikhail Gorbachev approach," which might best be characterized as "let's try capitalism." The slow and ambiguous transition in Russia left a mixed model in place, left time for doubts to fester about making the change, and left people to fight over dividing the economic pie rather than figuring out how to grow it. The same applies to making the conversion to EVA. Unquestionably the most important success factor is decisiveness. Making a swift, complete changeover is always the least risky strategy, and that takes leadership from the top. Otherwise, going to EVA is apt to be more arduous and less rewarding than it might be.

Inspiring and exemplary of these principles as it is, Federal-Mogul represents only one company, in one industry, based in one country. In truth, the right way to become an EVA company cannot be encapsulated in a single case. It is quite different for established organizations such as Federal-Mogul that must tear down and replace existing but outdated methods than it is for emerging mid-cap companies that have to install management systems in the first place. Implanting EVA into a successful company such as Eli Lilly or Hershey Foods requires quite a different tack than for firms like the former capital-squandering engine maker Briggs & Stratton. Large, diversified institutions like the German electrical giant Siemens require a multiyear effort even when that effort is moving ahead decisively. Cyclical firms such as Alcan or Millenium Chemicals present wholly different challenges from steady profit performers like Equifax or Centura Banks. Private firms, too, have special needs, particularly when the founding families are still involved. Utilities and other regulated companies such as the U.S. Postal Service have unique and particularly complex technical and social issues to resolve. While EVA is simple in concept, properly inculcating it into the systems, incentives, and culture of a company is always an imposing, subtle, and highly differentiated undertaking. But it also can be an exhilarating and extremely rewarding one.

This book began with the assertion that EVA represents a genuine revolution in management. It is a revolution because EVA is a new and fundamentally better answer to the age-old problem of how to align the interests of agents with principals, of how to bind managers and employees to the will of the shareholders. It works because it is an elegant and understandable way to create a web of overlapping ownership interests so that the wealth created by a company can be shared with all of the people who have helped to bring that wealth about. It works because at its best EVA represents the most socialistic form of capitalism.

Index

Index

Index

Index

Index